The Middle School Grammar Toolkit

Teaching grammar can be overwhelming and is often an overlooked part of effective instruction. *The Middle School Grammar Toolkit* to the rescue! Now in its second edition, this comprehensive guide makes grammar instruction fun and meaningful.

You will learn how to:

- Teach grammar in a practical and applicable way by presenting each grammar rule as a useful writing tool for students.
- Use mentor texts—excerpts from great literature—to help students understand grammar in action.
- Promote metacognition along the way, so that students become responsible for their own learning.
- Implement innovative instructional strategies and tools aligned with Common Core and other state standards.

Throughout the book, you'll find step-by-step recommendations for teaching grammatical concepts, such as understanding intensive pronouns, choosing language that expresses ideas precisely, forming verbs in different moods, and maintaining consistency in style and tone, and much, much more. Organized to help students meet the Common Core State Standards and other state language standards for Grades 6–8, the book includes tips addressing teaching for each of these grades, classroom snapshots that show you the tools in action, and specific instructional recommendations to engage students.

New! The second edition features revised classroom snapshots and exemplars to showcase successful practices, and new flowcharts to visually represent instructional recommendations. The expanded, free annotated bibliography is updated to include contemporary, high-quality young adult literature and gives examples of key grammatical concepts found in each work. These resources are available as Supplemental Downloads on our website.

Sean Ruday is an Associate Professor of English Education at Longwood University and a former classroom teacher. He frequently writes and presents on innovative ways to improve students' literacy learning. You can follow him on Twitter at @SeanRuday and visit his website at www.seanruday.weebly.com.

Other Eye on Education Books Available from Routledge

(www.routledge.com/eyeoneducation)

The Elementary School Grammar Toolkit, Second Edition
Using Mentor Texts to Teach Standards-Based Language and Grammar in Grades 3–5
Sean Ruday

The Common Core Grammar Toolkit
Using Mentor Texts to Teach the Language Standards in Grades 9–12
Sean Ruday

The First-Year English Teacher's Guidebook
Strategies for Success
Sean Ruday

Culturally Relevant Teaching in the English Language Arts Classroom
Sean Ruday

Matching Reading Data to Interventions
A Simple Tool for Elementary Educators
Jill Dunlap Brown and Jana Schmidt

Content Area Literacy Strategies that Work
Do This, Not That!
Lori G. Wilfong

Passionate Learners, Second Edition
How to Engage and Empower Your Students
Pernille Ripp

Passionate Readers
The Art of Reaching and Engaging Every Child
Pernille Ripp

Rigor in the K – 5 ELA and Social Studies Classroom
A Teacher Toolkit
Barbara R. Blackburn and Melissa Miles

From Texting to Teaching
Grammar Instruction in a Digital Age
Jeremy Hyler and Troy Hicks

Active Literacy Across the Curriculum
Connecting Print Literacy with Digital, Media, and Global Competence, K – 12
Heidi Hayes Jacobs

The Middle School Grammar Toolkit

Using Mentor Texts to Teach Standards-Based Language and Grammar in Grades 6–8

Second Edition

Sean Ruday

NEW YORK AND LONDON

Second edition published 2020
by Routledge
52 Vanderbilt Avenue, New York, NY 10017

and by Routledge
2 Park Square, Milton Park, Abingdon, Oxon, OX14 4RN

Routledge is an imprint of the Taylor & Francis Group, an informa business

© 2020 Taylor & Francis

The right of Sean Ruday to be identified as author of this work has been asserted by him in accordance with sections 77 and 78 of the Copyright, Designs and Patents Act 1988.

All rights reserved. No part of this book may be reprinted or reproduced or utilised in any form or by any electronic, mechanical, or other means, now known or hereafter invented, including photocopying and recording, or in any information storage or retrieval system, without permission in writing from the publishers.

Trademark notice: Product or corporate names may be trademarks or registered trademarks, and are used only for identification and explanation without intent to infringe.

First edition published by Routledge 2014.

Library of Congress Cataloging-in-Publication Data
Names: Ruday, Sean, author.
Title: The middle school grammar toolkit : using mentor texts to teach
   standards-based language and grammar in grades 6-8 / Sean Ruday.
Description: Second edition. | New York, NY : Routledge, 2020. | Includes
   bibliographical references. |
Identifiers: LCCN 2020004536 (print) | LCCN 2020004537 (ebook) | ISBN
   9780367435639 (hardback) | ISBN 9780367435622 (paperback) | ISBN
   9781003004141 (ebook)
Subjects: LCSH: English language—Grammar—Study and teaching (Middle
   school) | Common Core State Standards (Education)
Classification: LCC LB1631 .R844 2020 (print) | LCC LB1631 (ebook) | DDC
   428.0071/2—dc23
LC record available at https://lccn.loc.gov/2020004536
LC ebook record available at https://lccn.loc.gov/2020004537

ISBN: 978-0-367-43563-9 (hbk)
ISBN: 978-0-367-43562-2 (pbk)
ISBN: 978-1-003-00414-1 (ebk)

Typeset in Palatino
by Swales & Willis, Exeter, Devon, UK

Visit the eResources: http://www.routledge.com/9780367435622

Contents

Meet the Author — vii
Acknowledgments — viii
eResources — ix

Introduction "Grammar Tools": Helping Middle School Students Understand the Importance and Uses of Grammar — 1

Part I Grammatical Concepts Aligned with Grade 6 Common Core Language Standards — 13

1 Understanding the Impact of Intensive Pronouns — 15

2 Achieving Clarity with Proper Pronoun Case — 25

3 Using Punctuation to Set Off Nonrestrictive Elements — 36

4 Maintaining Consistency in Style and Tone — 48

Part II Grammatical Concepts Aligned with Grade 7 Common Core Language Standards — 61

5 Using Simple, Compound, Complex, and Compound-Complex Sentences — 63

6 Using Phrases and Clauses while Recognizing and Correcting Dangling Modifiers — 76

7 Choosing Language that Expresses Ideas Precisely and Eliminates Wordiness and Redundancy — 90

8 Distinguishing among Connotations of Words with Similar Denotations — 102

Part III Grammatical Concepts Aligned with Grade 8 Common Core Language Standards   **113**

9 Explaining the Functions of Verbals   **115**

10 Forming and Using Verbs in the Active and Passive Voices   **125**

11 Forming and Using Verbs in the Indicative, Imperative, Interrogative, Conditional, and Subjunctive Moods   **138**

12 Using Punctuation to Indicate a Pause or Break   **152**

Part IV Putting It Together   **165**

13 Assessing Students' Knowledge   **167**

Conclusion Final Thoughts and Tips for Classroom Practice   **175**

Annotated Bibliography   181
References   191
Appendix: Reproducible Charts and Forms You Can Use in
 Your Classroom   194

Meet the Author

Sean Ruday is an Associate Professor of English Education at Longwood University and a former classroom teacher. He frequently writes and presents on innovative ways to improve students' literacy learning. You can follow him on Twitter at @SeanRuday and visit his website at www.seanruday.weebly.com.

Acknowledgments

I would like to thank the wonderful teachers who welcomed me into their classrooms and made it possible for me to teach the lessons featured in the classroom snapshot sections of this book. I had a wonderful time working with these teachers and their amazing students.

I would also like to thank the students whose writings are included in this book. I am grateful to have worked with these talented and dedicated individuals, and am honored to feature their writings.

I am extremely appreciative of everyone at Routledge Eye on Education—especially Karen Adler and Lauren Davis—for their insight, guidance, and support.

I would like to thank my parents, Bob and Joyce Ruday. I am grateful for their encouragement in all aspects of my life.

Finally, I want to thank my wife, Clare Ruday. I can't imagine my life without the humor and happiness she brings to it.

eResources

The tools in the appendix can be downloaded, printed, and copied for classroom use. You can access these downloads by visiting the book product page on our website: http://www.routledge.com/9780367435622. Then click on the tab that says "eResources" and select the files. They will begin downloading to your computer.

Bonus: Along with the appendix tools, you'll find an annotated bibliography available for download. The bibliography lists high-quality young adult literature and gives examples of key grammatical concepts found in each work, so that you can use additional mentor texts with our students.

Introduction

"Grammar Tools": Helping Middle School Students Understand the Importance and Uses of Grammar

Standing in front of a room full of excitable seventh graders on a warm April day, I thought about the challenge before me. I had been asked by the school's principal to teach these students (and the others at the school) about grammatical concepts that aligned with the Common Core Standards. Ruth, the school's principal, wanted the students to not only understand these grammatical concepts, but also to be able to use them to improve the detail and clarity in their writings. "Our students just haven't mastered grammar," she explained to me. "They do (workbook) exercises and seem to know the material, but it eventually becomes clear that they don't know it well. We need to find a way to teach grammar to these children that makes them into better writers."

Faced with this task, I decided to begin teaching the students about grammar by activating an unexpected element of their prior knowledge: magic! I showed the class a book called *Houdini's Magic Coloring Book*. When you turn the pages of this book in a certain way, all of its pictures appear in black and white. However, when you turn the pages in a different way, all of the book's pictures appear in color. The students and I spent some time looking at the pictures in this book and talking about how different the color pictures look from the black-and-white ones. Once I was sure I had the students engaged, I transitioned to a discussion of grammar.

"Take a look at this sentence," I said to them, displaying a sentence on a piece of chart paper that read, "The boy ran inside." "What do you notice about it?"

"It tells you what the boy did," replied one student.

"That's true," I responded. "Does it have much detail?"

"No," answered another. "It's really basic. Not much detail."

"Very good," I replied. "Now, let's take a look at a revised version of this sentence." I turned to a new piece of chart paper, which read, "Since he was late for dinner, the boy ran inside."

"Now," I asked the students, "what do you notice about the detail in this version?"

"There's more information," stated one student.

"Yeah," another added, "now it says why he ran inside."

"Fantastic," I responded. "Even though these sentences tell us some of the same information—specifically, that the boy ran inside—this second sentence gives us more information. The first sentence I showed you is an example of a simple sentence, while the second sentence is called a complex sentence. When we talk about grammar together, we'll talk more about those sentence types, why writers use them, and how you can use them in your own writing to make your writing better."

The students nodded. The school's principal, who was in the back of the room watching this lesson, smiled at me, acknowledging this connection between grammar and effective writing, and I smiled back. "Now, I want you to think back to the pictures I just showed you from *Houdini's Magic Coloring Book*. The black-and-white pictures in the book are like simple sentences. The color ones are like the complex sentence we discussed: they provide a lot more detail and information. Many times, writers use the elements of grammar to give additional life or detail to basic sentences. Grammatical concepts are like tools writers use to make their writing more descriptive, clear, or interesting, just like a marker or paintbrush is a tool an artist can use to add more color to a picture."

As I finished this statement, one student interjected, "I never thought about grammar like that before." I nodded vigorously, knowing I had begun the process of preparing these middle schoolers to talk about grammar in insightful and meaningful ways.

This description of my work in a middle school classroom is meant to provide an introduction to the ideas and instructional methods described in this book. As the principal of this school indicated, many students do workbook exercises with grammar and learn it in other out-of-context ways, but very few learn the ways that grammatical concepts can drastically enhance the quality of a piece of writing. Research by Constance Weaver (1998) illustrates that grammar instruction presented through isolated exercises does little to improve the quality of students' writing, while grammar taught in the context of effective writing can enhance the quality of students' written works.

I decided to write this book to provide middle school teachers and administrators with a resource that would help them to teach their students key language standards in a way that improves the students' writing and enhances their awareness of how writers use specific grammatical concepts to make their pieces as strong as possible. This introductory chapter is divided into the following sections, each of which addresses a key element of this book's approach:

- A discussion of how grammatical concepts are important tools for effective writing.
- The importance of mentor texts to effective grammar instruction.
- The gradual release model of instruction.
- Key elements of middle school writing instruction.
- What to expect in the rest of the book, including the Common Core Language Standards in Grade 6–8 that this book addresses.
- A "What's New" section that describes the updates and features new to this second edition.

Grammar: A Set of Tools

Whenever I speak with students or fellow teachers about effective grammar instruction, I emphasize the relationship between grammatical concepts and tools. An effective writer uses each grammatical concept purposefully, just as a skilled craftsperson uses a tool with a clear understanding of the reasons for using it. In his book *On Writing Well*, William Zinsser (2006) explains, "Clear thinking becomes good writing: one can't exist without the other" (p. 8). I believe that this statement about clear thinking applies to effective grammar use: if an author clearly understands the use of a particular grammatical concept, that person will use it effectively. If the author's understanding of that concept is unclear or uncertain, it is less likely that the writer will use it well.

For example, the Grade 6 Common Core Language Standards address the use of intensive pronouns such as "myself" and "ourselves" (Common Core State Standards Initiative, 2010). In order for writers to effectively use this grammatical concept, they need to understand its purpose. In other words, they need to understand why one would use this "tool." Writers use intensive pronouns to add emphasis to a statement. For example, an author might have a character say "I will finish the project *myself*" rather than "I will finish the project." The intensive pronoun "myself" adds a level of emphasis to the sentence that the other version does not have. This type of pronoun is just one of the many grammar tools writers use to craft their works in the ways they desire. Just as a sculptor would use particular tools to turn a block of stone into a particular image, a writer uses specific elements of language to express a certain idea in a specific way.

In this book, each grammatical concept discussed is presented as a tool for effective writing. I believe that an integral part of learning about grammar is understanding how writers use specific elements of grammar in their works. When middle school students understand that writers use specific grammatical concepts in certain ways, they can begin to look at grammar differently, seeing it as a series of tools and skills that they can apply to their writing rather than a bunch of workbook exercises they need to complete for the sake of doing so. A seventh grader with whom I recently worked explained meaningful grammar instruction like this: "I always thought grammar workbooks were annoying and a waste of time. I didn't learn anything (from them). Talking about grammar as the tools of good writing makes grammar more useful, and I like that much better."

The Importance of Mentor Texts

In order for students to see grammatical concepts as tools that writers use to enhance their works, it is important to show them examples of published works in which writers use these concepts. These models are frequently called mentor texts because they show how published writers use particular concepts or strategies in their works and then guide the students as they apply these ideas on their own. Don and Jenny Killgallon (2010) explain that "Most authors learned to write through reading and imitating, at least to a certain extent" (p. 2). The idea of using mentor texts to teach students about grammar extends from the Killgallons' assertion that in order to teach students to effectively apply grammatical concepts to their own writing, they need to look at how professional authors use these concepts in theirs.

Another benefit of using mentor texts to teach grammar is the student engagement they can produce; with mentor texts, students can have craft-focused discussions about their favorite authors' works. When working with middle school students on the Common Core Language Standards and other rigorous state-based language standards, I always make sure to incorporate examples from literature that feature authors they enjoy, using particular grammatical concepts. The seventh-grade class I mentioned earlier in this chapter included many students who enjoyed Jeanne DuPrau's (2003) book *The City of Ember*, so I included the following complex sentence from that book in one of our conversations about that topic: "When Lina went to work the next morning, the street was oddly silent" (p. 84). By using a sentence from a high-interest text, I was able to spark the students' enthusiasm in the concept and get them to discuss grammar while also talking about one of their favorite writers.

Each chapter in my book contains examples of mentor texts: published works that show how professional authors use particular grammatical concepts. I have included these mentor texts to illustrate the many ways these concepts appear in the kinds of books that middle schoolers encounter. When I am trying to select grammar-focused mentor texts for middle schoolers, I use the following criteria: (1) Does this example clearly illustrate the grammatical concept I want my students to learn?; (2) Is this example from a text that is age- and reading-level-appropriate for my students?; and (3) Do I believe my students will be interested in this example? If I answer "yes" to all three of these questions, then I know the mentor text is one I will use.

The Gradual Release Model of Instruction

If your middle schoolers are anything like the ones I work with, you have surely noticed that they do not like to sit still for very long! Instead, they would rather be actively involved in the learning process. Fortunately, there is an instructional process that strategically combines active learning with direct instruction, called the gradual release of responsibility (Pearson & Gallagher, 1983). There are three parts to this process. First, teachers explain a particular concept or strategy to students, providing examples and describing the topic. Next, teachers work with the students on the focal concept, gauging their understandings and answering any questions. Finally, teachers "turn the students loose" to work on the concept independently, checking in with students individually as they apply the concept on their own.

While this method can work with a variety of subject areas, it is particularly applicable to teaching writing. Fletcher and Portalupi (2001) explain that this instructional method, when used most effectively, allows a writing classroom to take on the best attributes of an industrial arts, or "shop," class: students learn a particular skill or strategy and then spend the majority of the class period engaged in active learning, with the teacher providing individualized support when appropriate. The grammar instruction I describe in this book is based on the gradual release of responsibility model. I believe that grammar instruction, like other kinds of writing instruction, is most effective when students are actively engaged in their learning (and this is especially applicable to high-energy middle schoolers!). You will notice that the instructional recommendations I provide reflect the key elements of this instructional process: provide students with examples and an explanation of what a particular grammatical concept is and why it is important, work with them and gauge their understandings as they work on activities that focus on this concept, and finally turn the students loose as they apply this idea on their own (supporting them while they do so). While each set of instructional recommendations focuses on the specific elements of the grammatical concept being discussed, these fundamental "gradual release" elements stay consistent throughout, as they have been shown to be important parts of effective teaching (Fisher & Frey, 2003; Lloyd, 2004).

Key Elements of Middle School Writing Instruction

This book focuses on key grammatical concepts addressed in the Middle School Common Core Language Standards and other rigorous state standards. While the book is informed by concepts identified in the Common Core, these grammar tools are applicable to effective instruction whether or not a specific state adheres to the Common Core. Given the book's focus on middle school grammar and writing, it is important to address significant elements of middle school writing instruction and the ways that those attributes connect to teaching grammar effectively. In this section, I address the following elements of middle school writing instruction: (1) today's standards require middle schoolers to demonstrate increasing sophistication in language use; (2) today's standards require middle school students to read and write in a variety of genres; and (3) middle school students write to communicate in authentic ways.

Today's Standards Require Increasing Sophistication in Language Use

The Common Core Writing Standards and other revised and rigorous state standards call for students to demonstrate development in their language skills each year. For example, the Common Core Standards state that "Each year in their writing, students should demonstrate increasing sophistication in all aspects of language use" (Common Core State Standards Initiative, 2010). I found this statement particularly applicable to working with middle school students. As my students made the important transition into the middle school grades and progressed through those grades, I wanted to make sure that they showed continued understandings of grammatical concepts addressed in previous grades while also mastering the concepts specific to their current grade levels. Since the Common Core State Standards specifically state that "Students advancing through the grades are expected to meet each year's grade-specific standards and retain or further develop skills and understandings mastered in preceding grades" (Common Core State Standards Initiative, 2010), it was important to me to provide my students with in-depth grammar instruction that focused on grade-specific standards while also addressing any previous standards with which they struggled. While working with seventh graders, for example, I focused my instruction primarily on the language standards specific to that grade, but did not hesitate to also address any grammatical concepts associated with earlier grades with which they needed extra support.

Today's Standards Require Reading and Writing in a Variety of Genres

One especially noteworthy element of the Common Core State Standards and other updated and rigorous state standards is their call for students to read and write in a variety of genres—a requirement that relates to the reading, writing, and language standards. As students progress through their educational careers, they will need to read and write increasingly complex literary and informational texts. While doing so, the students will need to master increasingly complex elements of grammar and language in order to decipher challenging texts and compose their own works that contain insightful themes and strong arguments. In this book, I have included examples of grammatical concepts from a variety of middle-school-appropriate texts representing fiction and nonfiction. You'll encounter excerpts from graphic novels such George Takei's (2019) *They Called Us Enemy*, memoirs such as Trevor Noah's (2019) *It's Trevor Noah: Born a Crime. Stories from a South African Childhood. Adapted for Young Readers*, and a range of other fiction and nonfiction texts that incorporate a variety of perspectives and backgrounds. Examining grammatical concepts in this range of works and genres can ensure that students understand how a wide variety of writers use grammatical concepts to enhance their works. In addition, showing middle school students examples from this range of texts will meet the expectations that they work with a number of genres during literacy instruction.

Middle School Students Write to Communicate in Authentic Ways

To many middle school students, writing is more than just something they are assigned to do in school: it is a means of communication at a very social time in their lives. Middle school students value the way writing allows them to share honest emotions about high-interest topics and connect with their peers (Robb, 2010). When I teach grammar to middle schoolers, I work to capitalize on the social value of writing by demonstrating how grammatical concepts can help them to clearly convey their ideas. I explain that the tools of good writing are not only applicable to school, but rather to all forms of writing in which they engage. For example, when discussing the active and passive voice with a group of eighth graders, I asked the students about the different ways that they wrote outside of school and whether they typically used the active or passive voices when doing so. Some students discussed using text messages and Facebook posts to make weekend plans, while a few others talked about blogging about their favorite sports teams. The students explained which voices they used in their messages, posts, and blogs, and why. In this discussion, my students connected language standards and grammatical concepts to the kinds of writing that students use to communicate outside of school.

What to Expect in This Book

I have designed this book to be a guide for middle school English teachers interested in implementing effective and innovative methods of grammar instruction. The book uses the "toolkit" metaphor to discuss grammar instruction, describing each featured grammatical concept as a tool for good writing. I have organized the book into the following sections:

- ◆ Grammatical concepts aligned with Grade 6 Common Core Language Standards.
- ◆ Grammatical concepts aligned with Grade 7 Common Core Language Standards.
- ◆ Grammatical concepts aligned with Grade 8 Common Core Language Standards.
- ◆ A section on "Putting It Together," which contains a chapter on methods of formative and summative assessment that you can use to evaluate students' understandings of the grammatical concepts described in this book, as well as a concluding chapter, which contains final thoughts and tips for classroom practice.

In addition, available for download are the following items:

- ◆ An annotated bibliography, which lists the examples of young adult literature featured in this book, a key grammatical concept found in each work, and the Common Core Language Standard associated with that concept.
- ◆ An appendix, which contains easily reproducible graphic organizers and charts you can use when teaching your students about the grammatical concepts described in this book.

The following table lists the grammatical concepts described in the book, the chapters in which they are discussed, and the Common Core Language Standards with which they align.

Grammatical Concept	Chapter	Common Core Language Standard
Using Intensive Pronouns	Chapter 1	L6.1
Using Proper Pronoun Case	Chapter 2	L6.1
Using Punctuation to Set Off Nonrestrictive Elements	Chapter 3	L6.2
Maintaining Consistency in Style and Tone	Chapter 4	L6.3
Using Simple, Compound, Complex, and Compound-Complex Sentences	Chapter 5	L7.1
Using Phrases and Clauses while Recognizing and Correcting Dangling Modifiers	Chapter 6	L7.1
Choosing Language that Expresses Ideas Precisely and Eliminates Wordiness and Redundancy	Chapter 7	L7.3
Distinguishing among Connotations of Words with Similar Denotations	Chapter 8	L7.5
Explaining the Functions of Verbals	Chapter 9	L8.1
Forming and Using Verbs in the Active and Passive Voices	Chapter 10	L8.1
Forming and Using Verbs in the Indicative, Imperative, Interrogative, Conditional, and Subjunctive Moods	Chapter 11	L8.1
Using Punctuation to Indicate a Pause or Break	Chapter 12	L8.2

In order to make this book as clear and easy to use as possible, I have organized each chapter into the following sections:

- An overview of the key elements of the chapter's focal concept. This section provides a definition and key examples of the concept addressed in the chapter.
- A discussion of why the concept is important to good writing. This section explains why authors use this particular grammatical concept to enhance their works and includes mentor text examples to illustrate how the concept appears in published works.
- A "Classroom Snapshot." Each "snapshot" contains a description of my experiences teaching the chapter's focal concept to a middle school English class during my recent work as a grammar and writing instruction consultant at a middle school. I have included these "snapshots" so you can see how I taught my students about these grammatical concepts and learn from these concrete examples as you work with your students.
- Specific instructional recommendations. Each chapter contains specific recommendations for you to keep in mind when engaging your students in learning activities that focus on these concepts.

This book is designed to be practical and useful for your work as a middle school English teacher. Each chapter addresses what each concept is and why it is important for effective writing, but also provides specific descriptions and recommendations that are designed to help readers understand how to teach these concepts to their students. I want readers of this book to complete each chapter and think "I can do that in my classroom!"

What's New?

This book is a revised and updated edition of my 2014 book *The Common Core Grammar Toolkit: Using Mentor Texts to Teach the Language Standards in Grades 6–8*. In this new text, you'll find a number of new elements and features:

- Each chapter from one through to 12 contains flowcharts that visually represent the instructional recommendations described in that chapter. These flowcharts are designed to make the instructional processes discussed in the book visually appealing and even more accessible.

- The "Classroom Snapshot" sections have been made more concise in order to focus on the aspects of the described instruction that are most useful to readers.
- The mentor text examples throughout the chapters and in the Annotated Bibliography have been revised to include more contemporary texts from a wider and more diverse range of authors.
- In connection with the always-changing nature of the English language, I have added information that addresses the idea that pronouns are evolving, especially in the interest of being inclusive of all gender identities, and that teachers should continue to be aware of this evolution of language. I cited the National Council of Teachers of English's (NCTE) Statement on Gender and Language (2018) as a resource related to this topic.
- I changed the title from *The Common Core Grammar Toolkit: Using Mentor Texts to Teach the Language Standards in Grades 6–8* to *The Middle School Grammar Toolkit: Using Mentor Texts to Teach Standards-Based Language and Grammar in Grades 6–8, Second Edition*. This title change reflects the fact that the grammatical concepts discussed in this book are relevant to effective grammar and language instruction in all contexts, whether a school uses the Common Core State Standards or not. The Common Core Language Standards are similar to many other rigorous state standards and this book is designed to be useful to teachers in states and schools that both use and do not use the Common Core.

Now that you're oriented to the features and ideas in this book, let's get started! If you are ready to learn more about these grammatical concepts, why they are important to effective writing, and innovative ways to teach them, then keep reading!

Part I

Grammatical Concepts Aligned with Grade 6 Common Core Language Standards

Introduction

In Part I, we'll look closely at four grammatical concepts aligned with the Common Core Language Standards for Grade 6: intensive pronouns, pronoun case, nonrestrictive elements, and consistency in style and tone. In each chapter, we'll begin by examining the focal concept's features and then discuss its significance to effective writing. After that, we'll look at a snapshot of my experiences teaching the concept to a sixth-grade English class. I'll then share key recommendations to keep in mind when teaching your students about the chapter's focal concept before concluding with some final thoughts on the concept's importance and instructional strategies related to it.

The four concepts described in this section are tools that can enhance writing in specific and significant ways. Intensive pronouns, described in Chapter 1, are tools authors use to add emphasis to especially important statements. These words, such as "myself, yourself, himself, herself, itself, ourselves, yourselves," and "themselves," are used strategically in effective writing to make information stand out to readers. Pronoun case, described in Chapter 2, is a tool for clarity that ensures that the reader understands information in the way the author intended it. For example, a possessive pronoun used in a situation where there is no possession can confuse and distract readers; using it properly can help readers make sense of a text while avoiding distraction and confusion. The third concept described in this section, using punctuation to set off nonrestrictive elements from the rest of a sentence, is an important tactic for adding detail to writing in a clear and easy-to-understand way. By using this skill effectively, writers can incorporate details in their works that give readers extra information and help readers identify that information. This section concludes with Chapter 4, which discusses maintaining consistency in style and tone; this grammatical concept helps students think about the audience and purpose of a piece of writing and how the language choices that the author makes in the piece align with that audience and purpose. By applying this tactic to their own works, students can maximize the effectiveness of their writing and ensure that their works have the intended impacts on their audiences.

After reading these chapters, you'll have clear understandings of these grammar tools, why they're important, and how to put them into action in your classroom. Let's get started with our exploration of these important sixth-grade grammatical concepts!

A Note on Pronouns

Two of the chapters in this section discuss pronouns; it's important to keep in mind that pronouns are evolving, especially in the interest of being inclusive of all gender identities. As teachers, we should be aware of this evolution of language and keep it in mind as we work with our students. The National Council of Teachers of English's (NCTE) (2018) Statement on Gender and Language provides important insights and ideas on the evolution of language, suggesting that teachers

> frame instruction in grammar and usage conventions with ongoing discussion of the inherently dynamic and evolving nature of language, rather than asserting, implicitly or explicitly, that grammar and usage rules are timeless, universal, or absolute. Language shifts; make that part of the classroom conversation.

These conversations about the changing nature of language can address important inclusion-oriented aspects of pronoun use, such as the use of the pronoun "they" to refer to an unspecified singular antecedent and other pronoun uses that are inclusive of all gender identities and respectful of individuals' chosen pronouns. For example, the NCTE Statement on Gender and Language recommends using inclusive phrasing such as "Each cast member should know **their** lines by Friday" instead of binary-oriented phrasing such as "**his or her** lines."

Language is flexible and is always changing; we can use that flexibility to create classrooms that are safe and supportive for all students by incorporating developments in language and pronoun use to create an inclusive learning environment. For more information on this topic, I recommend reading the NCTE Statement on Gender and Language in its entirety. It can be found at www2.ncte.org/statement/genderfairuseoflang/.

1

Understanding the Impact of Intensive Pronouns

What Are Intensive Pronouns?

Common Core Language Standard 6.1 calls for students to "use intensive pronouns (e.g. *myself, ourselves*)" as part of a more general statement that students must "demonstrate command of the conventions of standard English grammar and usage when writing or speaking" (Common Core State Standards Initiative, 2010). Whether or not our teaching is directly connected to the Common Core, the concept of intensive pronouns is an important tool for our students to understand, as they can make a significant impact on a piece of writing. Intensive pronouns are words used to provide extra emphasis to a sentence by emphasizing a previously used noun or pronoun (Kolln & Funk, 2012). For example, in the sentence "The principal himself visited our class for lunch," "himself" is an example of an intensive pronoun. Note that the word "himself" is not needed for this sentence to make sense; the sentence "The principal visited our class for lunch" is perfectly fine grammatically. However, the intensive pronoun "himself" is still important to this sentence; it emphasizes that the principal was the one that visited our class and makes the impact of his visit apparent to the reader. In the sentence "I like pizza myself," the intensive pronoun "myself" emphasizes the fact that the speaker likes pizza. It indicates that while others may prefer different foods, that person enjoys pizza.

There are specific pronouns that can function as intensive pronouns in sentences; each of these is listed in Figure 1.1. In this figure, these pronouns are organized by person (first, second, or third) and number (singular or plural).

Person	Singular	Plural
First	myself	ourselves
Second	yourself	yourselves
Third	himself/herself/itself	themselves

Figure 1.1 Intensive Pronouns.

An important issue to note about intensive pronouns is that the words listed in Figure 1.1 do not always function as intensive pronouns. In other words, you might see one of these words in a sentence in which it functions as a different kind of pronoun. This is because the words that function as intensive pronouns can function as reflexive pronouns instead (depending on how they are used in a sentence). This is important to note because although this element of Common Core Language Standard 6.1 focuses specifically on intensive pronouns, a key aspect of understanding intensive pronouns is being able to differentiate them from reflexive pronouns. In the sentence "John saw himself in the mirror," "himself" is not used for emphasis, but rather to let readers know who John saw, making it a reflexive pronoun.

When I talk with students about identifying whether pronouns are reflexive or intensive, I encourage them to ask, "Does the sentence make sense without this pronoun?" If they answer "Yes," then they are identifying the pronoun as intensive, as that pronoun is used for extra emphasis but is not needed for the sentence to be grammatically correct. If they answer "No," then the pronoun must be reflexive because it notifies readers of key information that is needed for the sentence to be grammatically correct. For example, the sentence "Mr. Smith himself cooked dinner" contains an intensive pronoun; "himself" adds emphasis to the sentence but is not necessary. However, the sentence "Mr. Smith cooked dinner for his wife and himself" contains a reflexive pronoun; the sentence would not make sense if we eliminated the word "himself" from it.

Why Intensive Pronouns Are Important to Good Writing

Intensive pronouns are important tools for writers to have in their grammar toolkits. There are numerous situations in which writers might want to add an extra level of emphasis to a particular statement. For example, take the following passage from Hena Khan's (2017) novel *Amina's Voice*, in which

Amina Khokar, the book's narrator and protagonist, describes the difficulty that some people she knows have saying her name:

> Mama told me once that she picked my name thinking it would be easiest of all the ones on her list for people in America to pronounce. But she was wrong. The neighbor with the creepy cat still calls me Amelia after living next door for five years. And my last name? Forget about it. I could barely pronounce Khokar myself until I was eight.
> (p. 10)

In this excerpt, Amina uses the intensive pronoun "myself" to emphasize her feelings and experiences associated with her last name. This intensive pronoun affects the tone of the sentence in which it appears; without it, the sentence would not have the same impact as it currently does. With the intensive pronoun "myself" removed, that sentence would read "I could barely pronoun Khokar until I was eight." While this sentence conveys similar overarching information and makes sense grammatically, it does not emphasize Amina's experiences and perspectives the way that the version containing the intensive pronoun does. By including the intensive pronoun "myself," author Hena Khan skillfully maximizes the power of Amina's statement.

Intensive pronouns are important to both fiction and nonfiction writing. In the book *The Greatest Moments in Sports* (2009), author Len Berman uses an intensive pronoun to add emphasis to a description of an important moment in hockey star Wayne Gretzky's career. Berman recounts the game in which Gretzky broke the all-time points' record for National Hockey League players, which had been previously held by Gordie Howe, one of Gretzky's heroes. In this section, Berman notes that Howe was present at the game in which Gretzky broke his record and uses an intensive pronoun to emphasize this. After describing the details of the record-breaking goal, Berman states, "The crowd went wild. One of those on his feet was Howe himself" (p. 29). If Berman had not used this pronoun, the sentence would not have had the same effect on the reader that the current version does: it would read, "One of those on his feet was Howe." The intensive pronoun "himself" stresses the importance of Howe being present at Gretzky's achievement and helps readers grasp the significance of the information Berman describes.

So, why are intensive pronouns important to effective writing? As Khan and Berman's examples illustrate, these pronouns provide additional levels of emphasis to statements that call for it. While many statements do not require the emphatic effect of intensive pronouns, those that do can certainly be enhanced by this significant grammatical concept. The examples from *Amina's Voice* and *The Greatest Moments in Sports* described in this section utilize intensive pronouns to make sure specific statements have their desired effects.

 ## A Classroom Snapshot

As 28 boisterous sixth graders enter their English classroom and find their seats, I greet them and transition to the day's activity by stating, "You've been learning about pronouns, but today we're going to talk about a new kind—intensive pronouns. Intensive pronouns are used to add emphasis to a piece of writing, which can increase a statement's power and strength."

I direct the students to an easel pad in the front of the room. On a piece of paper on this easel pad, I have written the list of intensive pronouns found in Figure 1.1. "These are the intensive pronouns," I state. I explain to the students how they are organized by person and number like other pronouns they have studied. Once I have talked with the students about these fundamental elements of intensive pronouns, I transition to a discussion of how these pronouns are used in writing. "I call the intensive pronouns the 'emphasis pronouns' because they give additional emphasis to a statement. Let me show you an example." I turn the easel pad to a new sheet of paper, which contains the following sentence: "I finished cleaning the house myself." "This is an example of a sentence with an intensive pronoun," I explain. "Can anyone find it?"

Student hands go up around the room. I call on a young man who correctly identifies the intensive pronoun as "myself." "That's great," I respond. "This sentence uses the intensive pronoun 'myself' for extra emphasis. If we take the word 'myself' away, this sentence would say 'I finished cleaning the house.' That makes sense, but it doesn't have the emphasis that the original version does. Someone might say 'I finished cleaning the house myself' to emphasize that they did it without anyone helping. When we use intensive pronouns like 'myself,' we can make statements stronger or more powerful by putting additional emphasis on them."

After this, I inform the students that I am going to show them an example of an intensive pronoun from the book they are currently reading as a class—*The True Confessions of Charlotte Doyle* by Avi (1990). "This example I'll show you is from the part of the book where Charlotte is talking about washing her own clothes for the first time." I turn the easel pad to a piece of a paper that reads, "If I wanted to wash things—and I did try—I had to do it myself" (p. 67). I ask for any volunteers to identify the intensive pronoun in this sentence.

I quickly survey the raised hands and call on a student who says, "The intensive pronoun is 'myself.'"

"Great," I say. "Now, why do you think Avi, the author of this book, had Charlotte use an intensive pronoun in her narration here?"

"It gives more attention to her being the one to do it," explains a quick-to-reply student.

"That's right," I respond. "Using 'myself' here emphasizes Charlotte's statement that she was responsible for washing her clothes. If she said, 'I had to do it,' her statement wouldn't be as strong as 'I had to do it myself.'"

Following this discussion of these sentences, I transition the class to another activity in which the students will need to apply their knowledge of intensive pronouns. I tell them that their task is going to be to work with a partner and create a sentence with an intensive pronoun in it. I explain that once they are done, each pair will share its sentence, identify the intensive pronoun, and explain why that intensive pronoun is important to the sentence. I tear off the paper from the easel pad that lists the intensive pronouns, grouped by number and person, and post it on the whiteboard. "Use this chart as you work together to check your pronoun use," I explain. "I'll walk around the room and check in with you while you work."

The students work with their partners, creating sentences that contain intensive pronouns. I circulate around the room, checking in on different groups, and answering clarifying questions when needed. Once I have checked in with each group, I address the class: "It's time to hear from everyone. Each pair is going to read us its sentence, identify the intensive pronoun in it, and tell us why that pronoun is important."

A pair of female students volunteers to go first. "Our sentence is 'She made all of the cookies herself.' The intensive pronoun is 'herself' and it's important because it emphasizes that she made all of the cookies."

I praise these students' work, calling attention to the way they not only created a sentence with an effective intensive pronoun, but also the way they clearly identified it and explained its importance. After the other pairs also share their work, I commend the entire class: "You did an excellent job creating sentences with intensive pronouns and analyzing them! Tomorrow we'll think about how you can use intensive pronouns to enhance the pieces you're creating in writing workshop."

Recommendations for Teaching Students about Intensive Pronouns

In this section, I describe a step-by-step instructional process to use when teaching students about intensive pronouns. The instructional steps I recommend are: (1) show students sentences that contain intensive pronouns and discuss the pronouns' impact; (2) show students sentences with the intensive pronouns removed and discuss the differences; (3) have students work together to create sentences with intensive pronouns and reflect on their uses; and (4) ask students to look for ways to apply intensive pronouns to their own works. Since these steps are designed to help students apply their understandings of intensive pronouns, I suggest using the information at the beginning of this chapter (such as the chart in Figure 1.1 and the corresponding explanations) to ensure that students understand the fundamentals of intensive pronouns before beginning this instructional process.

1. Show Students Sentences that Contain Intensive Pronouns and Discuss the Pronouns' Impact

I recommend beginning this instructional process by showing students sentences that contain intensive pronouns and discussing the impact of those pronouns on the sentences. Doing so allows students to see what intensive pronouns look like in the context of an actual piece of writing (rather than examining them in isolation) and helps them to understand the importance of this grammatical concept to effective writing. I suggest showing students some examples from literature to illustrate how published authors use this grammar "tool." While many published examples can be effective ones to show students, I recommend utilizing examples from texts students have read or that are written by authors with whom they are familiar. This increased level of familiarity can increase students' engagement levels and facilitate their understandings of this concept. For example, in the lesson described in this chapter's classroom snapshot, I used an example from the novel *The True Confessions of Charlotte Doyle* for this purpose. Since the students were reading that book as a class at the time, my use of this example allowed them to connect the grammatical concept of intensive pronouns with a familiar text.

After you have shown students these examples, make sure you discuss with them the impact the intensive pronouns have on the sentences. If the sentence contains the intensive pronoun "myself," for example, talk with the students about why the author chose to include that pronoun and how it shapes the effect of the sentence. When you do this, you will help your students understand that authors use intensive pronouns to add emphasis to statements in their works. In the examples of intensive pronoun use in this chapter, each intensive pronoun is used to add emphasis to a statement by "intensifying" a previously stated noun or pronoun. For example, when discussing the intensive pronoun use in *The True Confessions of Charlotte Doyle*, one of the students pointed out the intensive pronoun "myself" "gives more attention" to the fact that Charlotte was the one who needed to wash her clothes. Observations such as this one indicate that students understand the uses of this grammatical concept.

2. Show Students Sentences with the Intensive Pronouns Removed and Discuss the Differences

After students have analyzed the importance of intensive pronouns in particular sentences, I recommend showing them the same sentences with the intensive pronouns removed and discussing the differences. This practice provides students with a visual illustration of how the sentence would look if the author did not incorporate that intensive pronoun, which can lead to increased awareness of the importance of this concept. To illustrate this, let us take the excerpt from *The Greatest Moments in Sports* previously mentioned in this chapter: "The crowd went wild. One of those on his feet was Howe himself" (p. 29). After showing middle schoolers this sentence and discussing the importance of the intensive pronoun "himself," I would then show students how the sentence would read without this intensive pronoun. I would display both the original version and the one with the pronoun removed and talk with them about the different kind of tone created by the adapted version. To help students understand this difference, I like to create a chart such as the one depicted in Figure 1.2. In this chart, I list the original sentence, the new version without intensive pronouns, and any insights the class has about the ways these sentences differ (a blank, reproducible version of this chart is available in the appendix).

Original Sentence	Sentence without Intensive Pronoun	How They Differ
"The crowd went wild. One of those on his feet was Howe himself" (p. 29).	The crowd went wild. One of those on his feet was Howe.	Without the intensive pronoun "himself," the second sentence does not have as much emphasis. The presence of this intensive pronoun allows that author to emphasize the fact that Gordie Howe was in attendance when Wayne Gretzky broke his record.

Figure 1.2 Sentences with and without Intensive Pronouns.

I like to do at least two examples of these with my students: one in which I do most of the analysis, and then at least one more in which they are responsible for the majority of the discussion of how the sentences differ. This helps me gradually release the responsibility of the activity to the students and gives them more ownership over their learning.

3. Have Students Work Together to Create Sentences with Intensive Pronouns and Reflect on Their Uses

The next step in this instructional practice releases even more of the responsibility onto the students by asking them to work in small groups to create sentences with intensive pronouns and then reflect on the uses of those pronouns. The classroom snapshot section of this chapter contains an example of this activity: I asked the students to work in pairs to create sentences with intensive pronouns, share those sentences, identify the intensive pronouns in them, and explain why those intensive pronouns are important to the sentences.

I feel this activity is beneficial on a number of levels. First, the students are working collaboratively while applying their knowledge of this grammatical concept. In addition, they are not only using the concept, but also reflecting on its importance. I believe that in order to effectively understand grammatical concepts, students need to think about why each concept is an important "tool" for good writing. As students consider the importance of different grammar "tools" and the reasons why writers use them, they will develop a deeper understanding of the importance of these grammatical concepts and be able to apply them to their own works. One way to facilitate this activity is to give the students a graphic organizer that is divided into three columns: (1) Sentence; (2) Intensive Pronoun; and (3) Why the Intensive Pronoun Is Important to the Sentence. If you feel your students need some extra support, model the activity using a sentence you have created, before asking them to create theirs. Figure 1.3 contains an example

Sentence	Intensive Pronoun	Why the Intensive Pronoun Is Important to the Sentence
The students themselves organized the entire school dance.	Themselves	It calls attention to the fact that the students were the ones that organized the dance. It is important because it emphasizes that the students were the ones that did it.

Figure 1.3 Model Sentence Analysis Chart.

of a model I have shown my students before asking them to work on this activity (a blank, reproducible version of this graphic organizer is available in the appendix).

4. Ask Students to Look for Ways to Apply Intensive Pronouns to Their Own Works

The final step in this instructional process is to ask students to look critically at their own pieces of writing for places to include intensive pronouns. It is important to advise students to use this grammatical concept cautiously; intensive pronouns should be used sparingly and only when the author really wants to add emphasis to a certain piece of writing. Despite these words of caution, intensive pronouns can be very effective tools that students can use to enhance their works. I recommend asking students to look at pieces of writing on which they are working and examine those pieces for any instances when an intensive pronoun could further emphasize a particular statement. While the students do this, I suggest holding one-on-one writing conferences with them in which the two of you discuss any situations in the student's writing that could be enhanced by an intensive pronoun and why an intensive pronoun would be appropriate to use in that situation. Remember to caution students against using these pronouns just for the sake of using them; we want our student writers to use this grammatical concept (as well as other concepts) strategically and with an understanding of its uses.

A student named Brody with whom I recently worked used an intensive pronoun to add emphasis to the opening line of a story he wrote. He was working on a piece about a young boy who wanted to explore in the wilderness like his older brothers had. His original piece read, "Even though Jack was from a family of outdoor explorers, he had never been on any explorations." When conferencing with me about ways to use intensive pronouns to enhance his writing, Brody revised the opening line of his piece to read, "Even though Jack was from a family of outdoor explorers, he had never been on any explorations himself." Note the addition of the intensive pronoun "himself" in this revised version, which emphasizes that Jack had not taken any of the explorations his family members had. When I asked Brody about this revised piece, he commented on the importance of the intensive pronoun he had added: "Adding 'himself' was good because it emphasizes that Jack hadn't been on any explorations yet. This is an important thing to emphasize because it's important to the story." Brody's analysis reveals his awareness of the emphasis added by the intensive pronoun "himself." Perhaps most impressive is his understanding of the importance of Jack's inexperience as an explorer to the story and the way this intensive pronoun emphasizes that fact for the reader.

Final Thoughts on Intensive Pronouns

- Intensive pronouns are included in Common Core Language Standard 6.1.
- Intensive pronouns are words used to provide extra emphasis to a sentence by emphasizing a previously used noun or pronoun (Kolln & Funk, 2012).
- If an intensive pronoun is removed from a sentence, that sentence will still be grammatically correct, but it will not have the same level of emphasis that it would have if the intensive pronoun is used.
- The intensive pronouns are: *myself, ourselves, yourself, yourselves, himself, herself, itself,* and *themselves*.
- The same words that are used as intensive pronouns are also used as reflexive pronouns.
- You can tell whether a pronoun is intensive or reflexive based on whether or not you can eliminate if from a sentence. If you can eliminate the pronoun and have the sentence still make sense (but lack emphasis), it is intensive.
- When teaching students about intensive pronouns:
  - Show students sentences that contain intensive pronouns and discuss the pronouns' impact.
  - Show students sentences with the intensive pronouns removed and discuss the differences.
  - Have students work together to create sentences with intensive pronouns and reflect on their uses.
  - Ask students to look for ways to apply intensive pronouns to their own works.

Figure 1.4 depicts this instructional process in an easy-to-follow flowchart.

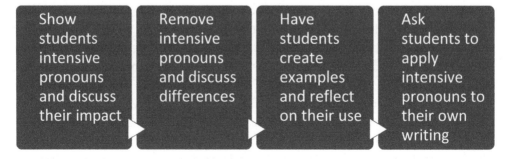

Figure 1.4 Intensive Pronouns Instructional Flowchart.

2

Achieving Clarity with Proper Pronoun Case

What Is Proper Pronoun Case?

Common Core Language Standard 6.1 calls for students to "Ensure that pronouns are in the proper case (subjective, objective, possessive)" (Common Core State Standards Initiative, 2010). In order for our students to use each of these pronoun cases properly, we will need to ensure they understand what subjective, objective, and possessive pronouns are and the situations in which they would use each one. In this section, we will explore each of these pronoun cases.

The Subjective Case

A subjective case pronoun is used when a pronoun is acting as the subject of a sentence. For example, let us take the sentence "Kate went running outside." "Kate" is the subject of this sentence, so a pronoun used in place of her name would be a subjective pronoun. In this case, the pronoun we would use would be "she," making our new sentence "She went running outside." "She" is one of the subjective pronouns, all of which are listed in Figure 2.1 and organized by person and number.

The Objective Case

An objective case pronoun is used when a pronoun is acting as an "object" in a sentence. The most common ways a pronoun can act as an "object" are by functioning as a direct object, an indirect object, or an object of preposition. It is important to understand what each one of these is in order to understand objective pronouns.

Person	Singular	Plural
First	I	we
Second	you	you
Third	he/she/it	they

Figure 2.1 Subjective Case Pronouns.

Direct Object

A direct object is a word or phrase that answers the question "whom?" or "what?" following a transitive verb (Kolln & Funk, 2012). For example, in the sentence "I saw George," the word "George" is the direct object because it tells us what the speaker saw. If we wanted to replace "George" with a pronoun, we would need to use a pronoun in the objective case since we would be replacing the direct object of the sentence. The sentence "I saw George," revised to replace "George" with a pronoun, would then read "I saw him," since "him" is the objective case pronoun used for a singular male.

Indirect Object

An indirect object is typically thought of as the recipient of a direct object (Kolln & Funk, 2012). For example, in the sentence "I made Lisa a sandwich," "Lisa" is the indirect object; she is the recipient of the sandwich (which is the direct object in this sentence). Since "Lisa" functions as the indirect object here, her name would be replaced with a pronoun in the objective case. "I made Lisa a sandwich," revised to replace "Lisa" with a pronoun, would read "I made her a sandwich," since "her" is the objective case pronoun used for a singular female.

Object of a Preposition

An object of a preposition is a noun or pronoun that follows a preposition and completes a prepositional phrase. For example, in the sentence "I stood beside Joe," "beside" is the preposition and "Joe" is its object. These two words work together to form a prepositional phrase. While "beside Joe" is a perfectly functional prepositional phrase, we might want to use a pronoun instead of Joe's name. In instances such as this, we would use an objective case pronoun because we would be replacing the object of a preposition. Since "him" is the objective case pronoun for a singular male, "I stood beside Joe," revised to replace "Joe" with a pronoun, would read "I stood beside him."

Figure 2.2 lists the objective case pronouns, organized by person and number.

Person	Singular	Plural
First	me	us
Second	you	you
Third	him/her/it	them

Figure 2.2 Objective Case Pronouns.

Person	Singular	Plural
First	my/*mine*	our/*ours*
Second	your/*yours*	your/*yours*
Third	his/hers/its	their/*theirs*

Figure 2.3 Possessive Case Pronouns.

The Possessive Case

Pronouns in the possessive case are used to show possession while taking the place of a noun. For example, let us take the sentence "Those are Bill's friends." We can substitute the possessive pronoun "his" for "Bill's," changing the sentence to "Those are his friends." Note that "his" replaces the noun "Bill" while still showing possession. Sometimes possessive case pronouns are used to replace not only the name of the person possessing the item, but also the actual item being possessed. For example, take a look at the following sentence: "That is the Smiths' house." We can substitute the possessive pronoun "their" to replace "the Smiths'," turning the sentence into "That is their house." However, possessive case pronouns can go one step further, as we can use the possessive pronoun "theirs" to eliminate the word "house" and turn the sentence into "That is theirs." In this sentence, the noun "house" is understood. Figure 2.3 lists the possessive case pronouns, organized by person and number. The possessive case pronouns such as "theirs" that can be used to replace both the person possessing an object and the object being possessed are italicized.

Now that we have explored the features of subjective, objective, and possessive case pronouns, let us discuss why being able to use them properly is important to effective writing.

Why Using Proper Pronoun Case Is Important to Good Writing

The ability to use proper pronoun case is an important skill for writers to possess, as it allows them to clearly express their thoughts and avoid confusing their readers. There are a variety of ways that using incorrect pronoun case can impact a piece of writing. First, incorrect pronoun case use can distract the reader from the message of the piece. If an author, intending to use a subjective pronoun and write "*I* went to Jack's birthday party," instead used an objective pronoun and wrote "*Me* went to Jack's birthday party," a reader might become distracted by this pronoun misuse and pay more attention to this mistake than to the actual information in the piece of writing. In addition, incorrect pronoun case use can confuse readers to the point where they might think the author is saying something different than what is actually intended. For example, if an author, intending to use an objective pronoun and write "At the party, I talked to *him*," mistakenly used a possessive pronoun and wrote "At the party, I talked to *his*," the reader's experience would be quite different. When reading the sentence with the possessive pronoun, a reader might think, "His what? His friends? His parents? Something else?" and assume that the author left out a word following the possessive pronoun "his." The use of proper pronoun case can avoid distraction and confusion and allow authors to clearly express important points.

To further illustrate the importance of pronoun case to high-quality writing, let us take a look at some examples from published works that feature the pronoun cases discussed in this chapter. These pronoun case mentor texts show proper use of these grammatical concepts and shed light on why using them effectively is important. First, let us focus on subjective pronoun use with the following sentence from Anthony Horowitz's (2000) novel *Stormbreaker*: "He took out a pair of Gap combat trousers, Nike sweatshirt and sneakers, got dressed, then sat on the bed and waited" (p. 33). In this sentence, Horowitz uses the subjective pronoun "he" to begin the sentence and ensure the reader understands that this pronoun is referring to the subject. If Horowitz mistakenly used an objective or possessive pronoun here, the sentence would not read as clearly. If the sentence used an objective pronoun, it would begin "*Him* took out a pair of Gap combat trousers…"; if it used a possessive pronoun, its opening would read "*His* took out a pair of Gap combat trousers…" Each of these sentences with incorrect pronoun case use would likely distract and confuse readers. By correctly using a subjective pronoun to represent the subject of the sentence, Horowitz ensures that his readers can clearly understand the situation.

Now let us look at how Horowitz correctly uses a possessive pronoun in *Stormbreaker*: in the sentence "Alex opened his eyes" (p. 32), Horowitz uses the possessive pronoun "his" to clearly demonstrate ownership. If this sentence read "Alex opened *he* eyes," as it would if it contained a subjective pronoun, or "Alex opened *him* eyes," which would be the case if it used an objective pronoun, readers would be confused by the mismatch between what the text says and what it should say. Correctly using this possessive pronoun provides clarity and eliminates any potential confusion.

Finally, let us examine how Horowitz uses objective pronouns in this novel. In the sentence "Nobody followed him" (p. 22), the pronoun "him" is the direct object in the sentence (it tells us whom or what nobody followed), so Horowitz correctly uses an objective pronoun to indicate this. If the author had instead used a subjective pronoun and wrote "Nobody followed *he*," readers would be distracted by this incorrect pronoun case use. If Horowitz wrote "Nobody followed *his*," the possessive nature of this pronoun would leave readers wondering exactly what nobody followed. As in the previous examples, Horowitz makes this sentence clear through effective pronoun case use.

As each of these examples from *Stormbreaker* illustrate, using proper pronoun case is an important part of effective writing. The subjective, objective, and possessive pronouns have different meanings and therefore are used differently in writing. In order for authors to create clear and easy-to-understand pieces, they must understand and properly use these grammatical tools. Now let us take a look inside a sixth-grade English classroom and see how these students worked on this important concept.

A Classroom Snapshot

As my sixth-grade English students take their seats and prepare for class to begin, I introduce them to the day's activity, explaining that they will work in pairs to select a book from the class library and find one of the types of the pronoun cases we have been studying. I then tell the students that once they find this example, they will share it with the class, identify the case in which the pronoun is written, and explain why the author used this particular case.

"Remember that all three parts of what you'll share are important," I explain. "It's important for you to identify a sentence with one of these pronoun cases and share it with the rest of us, but it's also really important for you to be able to tell us what case the pronoun is and explain why the author used that case. If you can do all three of these things, then you'll really show that you understand this important element of grammar."

I tell the students that before they begin, I want to show them an example of what I am asking them to do. "I'm going to share with a sentence from one of my favorite books, *Monster* by Walter Dean Myers (1999), and talk to you about an example of pronoun case in it. Pay attention, because after I do this, you'll do the same nd of thing with a book you and your partner select."

I explain to the students that I selected the sentence "I wouldn't lie in court" (p. 104) from *Monster*. I continue by identifying the pronoun case in this sentence and explaining why the author used that case: "The pronoun 'I' in this sentence is in the subjective case. Walter Dean Myers used a subjective

Sentence	Pronoun and Its Case	Why the Author Used that Case

Figure 2.4 Chart for Pronoun Case Analysis.

case pronoun here because 'I' in this sentence refers to the subject of the sentence. If he used a different pronoun case, like an objective or possessive case, it wouldn't make sense. He needed to use a subjective case pronoun because this pronoun refers to the subject."

"Before you start," I tell the students, "I want to show you a chart that you can use to help you with this activity." I show the students the chart depicted in Figure 2.4, placing it on the document camera and projecting it to the front of the classroom.

"As you can see," I inform the students, "this chart contains a space for the sentence you and your partner find, another space for you to write the pronoun you see and its case, and a third space for you to write why you think the author used that case. Even though you'll be sharing your work verbally, please fill out this chart while you're working because it will help you organize your ideas. I'm going to give each group a copy of this chart to use" (a reproducible version of this chart is available in the appendix).

"If I were to fill out this chart with the sentence from *Monster* I shared with you, I'd write 'I wouldn't lie in court' in here in the sentence space, I'd write 'I' and 'subjective' in the space for the pronoun and its case, and in the space for why the author used that case, I'd write that Myers used a subjective case pronoun because 'I' is referring to the subject of the sentence."

I ask the students if they understand what to do; a series of "yes" and "yeah" fill the room. I tell the students to get started by selecting a book from the classroom library. As the students descend on the collection of books in the room and select texts to use in this activity, I move around the room, handing each group a chart to fill out and answering any questions that students have. I check in with each pair of students, and then tell the class that it is time to hear from each of the groups. The student group that starts us off does an excellent job; both young men in the group stand up and one begins by saying, "We picked the book *Clockwork*, by Philip Pullman (1996). The sentence we picked was 'His expression was dark and gloomy.'"

The other group member then says, "The pronoun the author is using is 'his,' and it's in the possessive case. The author used a pronoun in the possessive case because this sentence is showing possession. 'His expression' shows that the expression belonged to a certain person (a guy named Karl) because it appeared on his face, so you need a possessive pronoun there."

Recommendations for Teaching Students about Proper Pronoun Case Use

In this section, I describe a step-by-step instructional process to use when teaching students about proper pronoun case use. The instructional steps I recommend are: (1) show students examples from literature of proper pronoun case use and discuss why the authors used those cases; (2) change the pronoun cases in examples from literature and discuss the differences with students; (3) ask students to find examples of pronoun case use in literature and analyze them; and (4) ask students to reflect on the pronoun case usage in their own writings. Since the steps of this process are designed to help students apply their knowledge of pronoun case usage, I suggest using the information at the beginning of this chapter (such as the explanations of subjective, objective, and possessive case pronouns and the corresponding charts in Figures 2.1, 2.2, and 2.3) to ensure that students understand the fundamentals of pronoun case use before beginning this instructional process.

1. Show Students Examples from Literature of Proper Pronoun Case Use and Discuss Why the Authors Used those Cases

I recommend beginning this instructional process by showing students examples from literature of proper pronoun case use and discussing why the authors used those cases. Doing this can help students grasp how using proper pronoun case is important to effective writing and understand that authors use these pronoun types purposefully based on the role a particular pronoun takes in a piece of writing. I suggest finding three sentences to show students: one that contains a subjective pronoun, one with an objective pronoun, and one with a possessive pronoun. Show each sentence individually to the students and talk with the students about what pronoun case is used and why the author used that case. For example, I might begin this activity by showing students the following sentence from Walter Dean Myers' (2001) memoir *Bad Boy*: "I traveled, mostly with Mama, to other parts of the city, but nothing matched Harlem" (p. 48). I would then identify "I" as a subjective case pronoun and think aloud about why Myers used this pronoun case, pointing out that "I" refers to the subject of this sentence and therefore the author would need to use a subjective case pronoun. After explaining the pronoun case use in this sentence, I would then show the students one that contains an objective pronoun and one that contains a possessive one. With each sentence, I suggest thinking aloud for the students about what pronoun case was used and why the author used it. Thinking aloud, an instructional strategy described in detail by Jeffrey Wilhelm (2001), is a practice in which teachers verbalize the way they are making sense of a particular text. While this strategy is often used to facilitate reading comprehension, I recommend using it when talking about how a published author uses a particular grammatical concept (in this instance, proper pronoun case). If we teachers make our thought processes transparent when considering why a published author used a particular grammatical concept in certain ways, we will help our students engage in this kind of analysis as well.

2. Change the Pronoun Cases in Examples from Literature and Discuss the Differences with Students

After you have shown students examples from literature of correct pronoun case use and discussed the reasons the authors used those cases, I recommend changing the pronoun cases in those same examples and discussing the differences with the students. For example, I would take the sentence from *Bad Boy* described in the previous section and change it from "I traveled, mostly with Mama, to other parts of the city, but nothing matched Harlem" to "*Me* traveled, mostly with Mama, to other parts of the city, but nothing matched Harlem." I would then ask the students to identify the pronoun case in the new version and explain what makes the original version correct and the new version incorrect. I recently showed these two sentences to a student with whom I was working and asked her to explain why Myers did not use "me" to begin this sentence. Much to my delight, this student replied, He used "I" instead of "me" because "I" is a subject pronoun and "me" is an object (pronoun). You would only use "me" if the pronoun was an object of something, and that's not what it is here. It's a subject.

I shouted, "Yes!," after this student completed her analysis, as I was thrilled by her explanation of why Walter Dean Myers used a subjective case pronoun in this sentence instead of an objective one.

3. Ask Students to Find Examples of Pronoun Case Use in Literature and Analyze Them

The next step in this instructional process is to ask students to find examples of pronoun case use in literature and analyze those examples. This step builds off of the instruction delivered in the first two parts of this process, but requires the students to take more of an active and independent role in their learning by doing the following: (1) selecting a piece of young adult fiction or nonfiction; (2) looking through that piece to find an example of at least one of these pronoun cases; (3) identifying the pronoun used in that example and the case in which it is written; and (4) explaining why the author chose to use that particular case. I like to ask students to complete this step in small groups because I believe they benefit from working together to find and analyze the examples of pronoun case usage.

This chapter's classroom snapshot contains a description of a group of sixth graders working on this activity in pairs. Before the students did this activity on their own, I modeled it for them using a sentence from the novel *Monster* that contains the subjective pronoun "I." Research findings (such as those by Harvey & Goudvis, 2007) indicate that students benefit from seeing their teachers model activities before doing them on their own. Because of this, I recommend modeling this activity for your students before asking them to complete it on their own. Demonstrating how to identify, label, and analyze the pronoun case use in a passage before asking students to do so on their own can show students how to navigate it on their own and give them confidence while they do so.

4. Ask Students to Reflect on the Pronoun Case Usage in Their Own Writings

The final step in this instructional process is to ask students to examine their own written works and reflect on the pronoun case usage in them. To do this, I recommend conferencing with each student and asking the student to locate a subjective, objective, or possessive case pronoun in a piece of writing. After this, ask the student to explain to you why one would use that pronoun instead of one of the other cases. For example, if a student shows you an example of an objective case pronoun, ask the student to tell you why this pronoun was the right fit for that situation instead of a subjective or possessive one.

I like this step because it asks the students to conduct analyses similar to those they have been completing throughout this process, but with a twist: instead of analyzing a piece of literature, they are now applying those same analytical tools to their own writing. By analyzing their own pronoun case use, the students can understand that this grammatical concept is a tool that they need to strategically apply to their own writing in order for their written works to be as strong as possible. When recently conducting this activity, I spoke with a student who identified a possessive pronoun in his writing and provided an insightful observation of why he used that kind of pronoun instead of one of the other cases:

I was writing about my hockey stick, so I had to use "my," a possessive pronoun, when I was writing about it because I was showing that it belonged to me. The other pronoun cases don't show possession, so this was the one that would be right to use.

Final Thoughts on Proper Pronoun Case

- The use of proper pronoun case is addressed in Common Core Language Standard 6.1.
- The three specific cases addressed in this standard are the objective, subjective, and possessive cases.
- A subjective case pronoun is used when a pronoun is acting as the "subject" of a sentence.
- An objective case pronoun is used when a pronoun is acting as an "object" in a sentence. The most common ways a pronoun can act as an "object" is by functioning as a direct object, an indirect object, or an object of preposition.
- A possessive case pronoun is used to show possession while taking the place of a noun.
- The ability to use proper pronoun case is an important skill for writers to possess, as it allows them to clearly express their thoughts and avoid confusing their readers.
- Incorrect pronoun case use can distract the reader from the message of the piece and can even confuse readers to the point where they might think the author is saying something different than what is actually intended.
- When teaching students about proper pronoun case:
  - Show students examples from literature of proper pronoun case use and discuss why the authors used those cases.
  - Change the pronoun cases in those examples and discuss the differences with students.
  - Ask students to find examples of pronoun case use in literature and analyze them.
  - Ask students to reflect on the pronoun case usage in their own writings.

Figure 2.5 depicts this instructional process in an easy-to-follow flowchart.

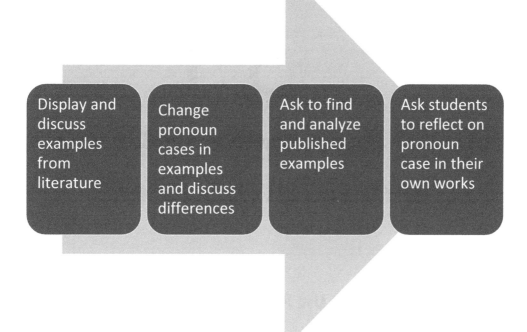

Figure 2.5 Pronoun Case Instructional Flowchart.

3

Using Punctuation to Set Off Nonrestrictive Elements

What Does It Mean to Use Punctuation to Set Off Nonrestrictive Elements?

Common Core Language Standard 6.2 calls for students to "Use punctuation (commas, parentheses, dashes) to set off nonrestrictive/parenthetical elements" as part of a more general requirement that students "Demonstrate command of the conventions of standard English capitalization, punctuation, and spelling when writing" (Common Core State Standards Initiative, 2010). The ability to use punctuation in this way is an important aspect of effective writing regardless of one's connection to the Common Core, as it helps facilitate clear communication.

In this section, we will explore what it means for students (and all other writers) to do this in their works. There are two key topics to understand when exploring this standard: (1) what nonrestrictive elements are; and (2) how to use punctuation to set these elements off from the rest of a sentence. Let us look at each of these topics in more detail.

Nonrestrictive Elements

Nonrestrictive (or parenthetical) elements are groups of words that provide additional information to a sentence, but are not essential to its meaning. For example, in the sentence "George, the best player on the team, was injured during the first half of the soccer game," "the best player on the team" is an example of a nonrestrictive element. It gives the reader additional information about George that, while useful, is not essential to the sentence's meaning. Another example of a nonrestrictive element is found in the sentence

"My children, three rambunctious boys, keep me busy every day." In this sentence, "three rambunctious boys" is a nonrestrictive element; it provides additional detail, but is not necessary to the sentence's meaning. Without this additional element, the sentence would read "My children keep me busy every day." Now, it is on to the next step of understanding this standard: exploring how to use punctuation to set these elements off from the rest of a sentence.

How to Use Punctuation to Set Off Nonrestrictive Elements

Whenever writers use a nonrestrictive element, they need to separate it from the rest of the sentence using punctuation. As Common Core Standard 6.2 states, commas, parentheses, and dashes are three forms of punctuation used to set off nonrestrictive elements. No matter which punctuation type is used, the guidelines for using punctuation to separate a nonrestrictive element from the rest of the sentence remain the same: the author must use punctuation to clearly set the nonrestrictive element apart from the rest of the sentence. Many nonrestrictive elements function as "sentence interrupters" because they interrupt the rest of the sentence to provide some additional detail. In situations such as this, the same punctuation must come before and after the nonrestrictive element that interrupts the rest of the sentence. Recall the example "My children, three rambunctious boys, keep me busy every day" used in the previous section; when creating this sentence, I inserted a comma before the nonrestrictive element "three rambunctious boys" and then another one following it. I could have also chosen to use parentheses or dashes in place of these commas, allowing the sentence to read "My children (three rambunctious boys) keep me busy every day" or "My children—three rambunctious boys—keep me busy every day." Any of these options would be grammatically correct and would clearly identify "three rambunctious boys" as a nonrestrictive element in the sentence. In addition to providing detail in the middle of sentence, nonrestrictive elements can also have other placements, such as at the sentence's end. For example, the previous sentence could be revised to read "I am always kept busy by my children—three rambunctious boys." This new version still contains the same nonrestrictive element of "three rambunctious boys," but includes that information at the sentence's end instead of in the middle.

Why Using Punctuation to Set Off Nonrestrictive Elements Is Important to Good Writing

It is important that writers use punctuation to set off nonrestrictive elements in their works, as doing so clearly separates this additional information from the rest of the sentence. If writers did not use punctuation to differentiate between nonrestrictive elements and the rest of a sentence, it could be difficult for readers to determine which part of a sentence is included to provide additional information and which is essential to the sentence's meaning. In this section, we will take a look at how published author Gayle E. Pitman uses punctuation to set off nonrestrictive elements in one of her works and explain the significance of each example.

In her 2019 book *The Stonewall Riots: Coming Out in the Streets*, Gayle E. Pitman uses commas, parentheses, and dashes to set off nonrestrictive elements in sentences. This nonfiction text describes the Stonewall Riots of 1969, a series of demonstrations by members of the LGBTQ+ community in response to a police raid of the Stonewall Inn in New York City, as well other important events and individuals in American gay history. When introducing activist Rita Mae Brown to the reader, Pitman uses commas to separate contextual details about Brown's identity from the rest of the sentence: "Rita Mae Brown, a lesbian who also identified as a feminist, had difficulty finding a group that addressed all aspects of her identity" (p. 135). Pitman presents her description of Brown as "a lesbian who also identified as a feminist" as a nonrestrictive element in the middle of the sentence that provides contextual detail developing the reader's understanding. By using commas to separate this information from the rest of the sentence, Pitman ensures that readers can differentiate between these details and the rest of the sentence and clearly identify it as additional context meant to develop the reader's understanding. Since this nonrestrictive element is separated from the rest by the commas, its role in the sentence is clearly communicated to the reader.

At another point in the book, Pitman uses parentheses to set a nonrestrictive element off from the remainder of a sentence. When describing another police raid of an establishment frequently attended by gay individuals (the Tay-Bush Inn in San Francisco), Pitman writes "In the end, 103 people (89 men and 14 women) were arrested and taken to jail" (p. 22). Pitman's use of these parentheses shows readers that this information is a "sentence interrupter" meant to provide additional information to readers regarding the male–female breakdown of the arrests. Just as with the previous example about Rita Mae Brown, Pitman's use of this punctuation is important because it eliminates any potential confusion about the role of the restrictive element in this sentence. By separating "89 men and 14 women" from the rest of the sentence with parentheses, she clarifies to readers that this is an additional piece of information that provides extra detail to the sentence.

Pitman uses a dash to separate a nonrestrictive element when describing the events of the Stonewall Riots and a chant of "gay power" that caught on during the events. After explaining that people in the Stonewall Inn chanted "gay power," Pitman states "The person who led the chant was Craig Rodwell, a gay activist and owner of the Oscar Wilde Memorial Bookshop—the first gay bookstore in the United States" (p. 69). In this sentence, the nonrestrictive element "the first gay bookstore in the United States" is separated from the rest of the sentence with punctuation to convey that it provides additional context and information that, while informative, is separate from the main part in the sentence. The use of this dash provides clarity to the reader by distinguishing between the nonrestrictive element and the rest of the sentence.

As these three examples illustrate, the act of using punctuation to separate nonrestrictive elements from the rest of a sentence is an important element of effective writing. Gayle E. Pitman uses this grammatical tool to add detail to her sentences while also ensuring that readers understand which parts of the sentence represent additional contextual details and which are essential to the sentence's meaning. In the next section, we will take a look inside a sixth-grade classroom and see some middle schoolers apply their knowledge of using and punctuating nonrestrictive elements.

A Classroom Snapshot

I begin today's class by telling my students, "we've been talking about using punctuation to set off nonrestrictive elements from the rest of a sentence, but today we're going to do something new with this same topic. I'm going to ask you and your partner to pick a book from the class library, find a sentence that *doesn't* have a nonrestrictive element, and add one to it."

I explain to the students that there are a few ideas that they will need to remember and place the information in Figure 3.1 on the document camera, projecting it to the front of the classroom.

Tips for Using and Punctuating Nonrestrictive Elements

1. Nonrestrictive elements add extra information to sentences.

2. You can remove a nonrestrictive element from a sentence and see that the sentence still makes sense.

3. Nonrestrictive elements can be separated from the rest of the sentence by commas, parentheses, or dashes.

4. If a nonrestrictive element "interrupts" a sentence, the same punctuation must be used before and after the element to separate it from the remainder of the sentence.

Figure 3.1 Tips for Using and Punctuating Nonrestrictive Elements.

I review this information with the students, reminding them of some examples I showed them in the preceding classes. Once I have reviewed this information and I am comfortable with the students' understanding of it, I tell them it is time for them to get to work: "Your job," I tell them, "is to work with your partner and do the following things: first, pick a book from the classroom library. Second, find a sentence in that book that doesn't have a nonrestrictive element. Third, add a nonrestrictive element to the sentence, paying attention to how you'd punctuate the sentence with that nonrestrictive element in it. When it's time to share, I'm going to ask each group to read the original sentence you found and then tell me the way you revised it to include a nonrestrictive element. When you tell me the way the sentence would look with the nonrestrictive element, I want you to also tell me all of the punctuation that should go in that sentence. I'll write it on the board exactly how you tell me to, including the punctuation you recommend."

The students begin working and I move around the room, checking in with them and discussing how they are doing. One thing that especially impresses me is the variety of punctuation the students are using. While some are using commas, others are using dashes and parentheses for this purpose. Since these students have said they are not especially familiar with using dashes and parentheses in writing, I am thrilled to see them trying out these punctuation forms.

I meet with one group that is using Wendy Mass' (2004) novel *Leap Day* for this activity and ask them how they are progressing. "We've found our sentence," one member of the group says, "and we think we know what nonrestrictive element we want to add."

"That's great," I reply. "What is the sentence and what is the element?"

"The sentence is 'Ms. Conners takes her seat and slowly scans around the circle, meeting everyone's eyes'" (p. 89), responds the other group member. "Josie, one of the characters in the book, really likes her teacher, Ms. Conners, so the nonrestrictive element we want to add is 'who is a really cool teacher.'"

"Fantastic," I respond. "Have you thought about how you'd punctuate the sentence with that nonrestrictive element added?"

"We want to use dashes," answers the student.

"A great choice," I tell them. "Dashes can really make a nonrestrictive element stand out."

After I meet with more students, I call the class back together and remind them of the procedures for sharing their work, emphasizing that it is important that the group states not only what nonrestrictive element they would add to their original sentence, but how they would punctuate that sentence.

One pair quickly volunteers to share its work, with one student explaining, "We used *My Brother Sam is Dead* (Collier & Collier, 1974). The original sentence we picked out was 'My father shook his head.' We added 'the wisest man I know' for the nonrestrictive element."

"Good job," I tell them. "Now, you tell me how to punctuate it and I'll write that new sentence on the board."

"Okay," responds the student. "Well, you'd start with the word 'My,' with the 'm' capitalized."

"Good," I say, encouraging his effort and attention to detail.

"And then 'father.' After 'father,' start a parentheses, then write 'the wisest man I know,' and then end the parentheses. And then, the words 'shook his head,' with a period at the end."

"Wonderful work, I like how you used parentheses there, and you did a great job of remembering to close those parentheses." I point to the sentence on the board and say, "This a great example of how to punctuate a sentence with a nonrestrictive element in it."

Recommendations for Teaching Students to Punctuate Nonrestrictive Elements

In this section, I describe a step-by-step instructional process to use when teaching students to punctuate nonrestrictive elements. The instructional steps I recommend are: (1) show students examples from literature of how authors use and punctuate nonrestrictive elements; (2) show students those same examples without nonrestrictive elements; (3) ask students to add nonrestrictive elements to sentences from literature that do not include them; (4) ask students to incorporate nonrestrictive elements into their writing; and (5) have students reflect on the impact and punctuation of the nonrestrictive elements they added. Since these steps are designed to help students apply their understandings of punctuating nonrestrictive elements, I suggest using the information in the beginning of this chapter about what nonrestrictive elements are and how to punctuate them to ensure that students understand the fundamentals of this concept and its punctuation before beginning this instructional process.

1. Show Students Examples from Literature of How Authors Use and Punctuate Nonrestrictive Elements

The first step in this instructional process is to show students examples of how published authors use and punctuate nonrestrictive elements in their own works. Providing students with these examples has two key benefits: first, it clearly demonstrates the ways nonrestrictive elements can add important details to a piece of writing; second, it illustrates the proper punctuation of nonrestrictive elements, allowing students to see correct punctuation in a published text rather than in a grammar workbook or a series of out-of-context exercises. Since Common Core Standard 6.2 calls for students to be able to use commas, parentheses, and dashes for this purpose, I recommend showing students examples from published works that use each one of these punctuation forms to separate nonrestrictive elements from the rest of a sentence. The three examples from Gayle E. Pitman's *The Stonewall Riots: Coming Out in the Streets* described earlier in this chapter are excellent options for this activity (and align with the Common Core Standards' expectation that students read informational texts in addition to literature). For example, if you showed your students the sentence "In the end, 103 people (89 men and 14 women) were arrested and taken to jail," you would want to emphasize the way the author uses the nonrestrictive element "89 men and 14 women" to include additional information about the arrested individuals, but you would also want to be sure to point out the way that the author punctuates this nonrestrictive element, specifically calling attention to the way she uses a comma before and after the element to ensure that readers understand that this element is used to provide the sentence with extra detail. While Pitman's sentence is a strong example of an author's use of a nonrestrictive element, I also encourage you to keep in mind your students' interests and reading levels when selecting mentor texts that you will use to demonstrate this grammatical concept.

2. Show Students Those Same Examples without Nonrestrictive Elements

Once you have shown students sentences from published works and talked with them about the authors' use and punctuation of nonrestrictive elements, I encourage you to next show your students those same sentences without the nonrestrictive elements used. When I do this with my students, I not only point out the different amount of detail in the new sentence, but also the change in its punctuation. Figure 3.2 contains the examples from *The Stonewall Riots: Coming Out in the Streets* previously featured in this chapter, but this time with a new feature: each sentence is listed in its original form as well as in a revised form that no longer includes the nonrestrictive element.

By showing students original published sentences that contain nonrestrictive elements as well as revised versions that do not, you can help your students clearly see the differences between them—both in the content and the punctuation of the sentences. Providing students with these concrete "before and after" examples can help them further understand the impact of nonrestrictive elements, as well as the ways authors use commas, parentheses, or dashes to clearly distinguish them.

Original Sentence	Sentence without Nonrestrictive Element
"Rita Mae Brown, a lesbian who also identified as a feminist, had difficulty finding a group that addressed all aspects of her identity" (p. 135).	Rita Mae Brown had difficulty finding a group that addressed all aspects of her identity.
"In the end, 103 people (89 men and 14 women) were arrested and taken to jail" (p. 22).	In the end, 103 people were arrested and taken to jail.
"The person who led the chant was Craig Rodwell, a gay activist and owner of the Oscar Wilde Memorial Bookshop—the first gay bookstore in the United States" (p. 69).	The person who led the chant was Craig Rodwell, a gay activist and owner of the Oscar Wilde Memorial Bookshop.

Figure 3.2 Sentences with and without Nonrestrictive Elements.

3. Ask Students to Add Nonrestrictive Elements to Sentences from Literature that Do Not Include Them

This activity, described in detail in the classroom snapshot section of this chapter, requires students to take an active role while learning about using and punctuating nonrestrictive elements. When I do this activity with students, I ask them to select a text from the classroom or school library, find a sentence that does not contain a nonrestrictive element, and add a nonrestrictive element to that sentence. This gives students experience adding relevant nonrestrictive elements to sentences and punctuating them. They must look carefully at the published text they use in order to determine what kind of nonrestrictive element would be appropriate to add to that work and then decide what kind of punctuation to use when adding it. When I did this activity in the sixth-grade class described in the classroom snapshot section, I asked each small group to read me the original sentence and then tell me exactly how that sentence would read if it were revised to include a nonrestrictive element, including the punctuation that they would add to the sentence. I have found that asking the students to include the punctuation that they would use with the nonrestrictive element further solidifies for them the importance of using properly punctuated nonrestrictive elements when writing.

It can be beneficial to give students a graphic organizer to complete while working on this activity, such as the one depicted in Figure 3.3, which asks

Original Sentence	Sentence Revised to Include Nonrestrictive Element	Nonrestrictive Element You Added	Punctuation Used with Nonrestrictive Element

Figure 3.3 Graphic Organizer for Adding Nonrestrictive Elements.

students to write the original sentence, create a revised sentence with a nonrestrictive element, and then specifically identify the nonrestrictive element used and the punctuation used along with it (this graphic organizer can also be found in the appendix). Asking students to include all of this information can help them clearly identify the changes they made to the original sentences and can ultimately help them apply these skills to their future writing.

4. Ask Students to Incorporate Nonrestrictive Elements into Their Writing

The next step in this instructional process is to ask students to incorporate nonrestrictive elements in their own written works. While doing this, students will need to pay attention to the information added by the nonrestrictive element as well as the punctuation used to distinguish it from the remainder of the sentence. At this point in the instructional process, the students have seen examples of sentences with and without nonrestrictive elements and have practiced adding these elements to sentences they have found in literature, so they are now ready to apply this grammatical concept to their own works. When I ask my students to do this, I give them two pieces of advice. First, I tell them to only add nonrestrictive elements to statements that might benefit from some extra detail. Every sentence certainly does not require one of these to be added to it, but some, such as the examples from Gayle E. Pitman's work, can be enhanced with the information nonrestrictive elements can provide. Second, I advise them to be sure to use commas, parentheses, or dashes to clearly set the nonrestrictive element off from the rest of the sentence and show the reader that this element is used to provide additional detail.

Figures 3.4 and 3.5 contain excerpts from a story written by a student named Brody that show how student writing can be enhanced with the inclusion of nonrestrictive elements. The text in Figure 3.4 is from the original

> **Jack set up his tent and crawled inside. "So, this is what's like to be in the wilderness," he said to himself. Jack stared at the moon and then began to howl at it. He knew he needed to sleep, but he just wanted to stay up and howl at the moon.**

Figure 3.4 Original Excerpt from Brody's Story.

> **Jack set up his tent, a small and worn out red thing he found in his dad's shed, and crawled inside. "So, this is what's like to be in the wilderness," he said to himself. Jack stared at the moon—which he'd never done before—and then began to howl at it. He knew he needed to sleep (he was planning a big hike for tomorrow), but he just wanted to stay up and howl at the moon.**

Figure 3.5 Excerpt Revised to Include Nonrestrictive Elements.

draft of his story about a boy who wants an adventure in the wilderness, while the text in Figure 3.5 shows how the story read after Brody revised it to include nonrestrictive elements. I include both excerpts here to show how this student enhanced his work by revising it to include this grammatical concept.

 These excerpts from Brody's story show the important details that can be provided through the use of nonrestrictive elements and the importance of punctuating them clearly. For example, Brody's use of the nonrestrictive element "he was planning a big hike for tomorrow" provides context for Jack's feeling that he needed to sleep, while the parentheses surrounding this statement identify it as a nonrestrictive element.

5. Have Students Reflect on the Impact and Punctuation of the Nonrestrictive Elements They Added

The final step in this instructional process is to ask students to reflect on the nonrestrictive elements they added to their works and the ways they punctuated those elements. To do this, I recommend asking students to examine the nonrestrictive elements they added to their existing writing and then answer the following questions:

1. What information did that nonrestrictive element add? Why is that information important?
2. How did you punctuate that nonrestrictive element? Why is the punctuation of this nonrestrictive element important?

When students answer these questions, they are forced to think critically about the impact of the nonrestrictive element they identified and the importance of its punctuation. This reflection process requires students to think of nonrestrictive elements (and their punctuation) as an aspect of effective writing that authors use purposefully. I like to ask students to answer these questions individually in writing and then share their responses with a partner or small group. As the students share those responses, I will listen to their ideas and then ask if anyone is interested in sharing with the whole class.

When Brody shared his reflections on the writing sample depicted in Figure 3.5, he picked out the nonrestrictive element "which he'd never done before" and said, "It's important because it shows that looking at the moon is something new for Jack." When commenting on his use of dashes to set off this nonrestrictive element, Brody explained, "(Using dashes) is one way to show that this is extra information." By reflecting on the nonrestrictive elements that they use in their writing and the way they punctuate them, students such as Brody can think about the importance of this grammatical tool to effective writing and the way punctuating it clearly can help achieve its desired effect.

Final Thoughts on Using and Punctuating Nonrestrictive Elements

- ◆ The use of punctuation to set off nonrestrictive/parenthetical elements is addressed in Common Core Language Standard 6.2.
- ◆ Nonrestrictive (or parenthetical) elements are groups of words that provide additional information to a sentence, but are not essential to its meaning.

- Whenever writers use nonrestrictive elements, they need to separate those elements from the rest of the sentence using punctuation to show that the nonrestrictive element represents extra detail.
- Three types of punctuation used to separate a nonrestrictive element from the rest of a sentence are commas, parentheses, and dashes.
- If a nonrestrictive element "interrupts" a sentence by providing additional detail in the middle of it, the same punctuation must come before and after the nonrestrictive element.
- When teaching students to punctuate nonrestrictive elements:
  - Show students examples from literature of how authors use and punctuate nonrestrictive elements.
  - Show students those same examples without nonrestrictive elements.
  - Ask students to add nonrestrictive elements to sentences from literature that do not include them.
  - Ask students to incorporate nonrestrictive elements into their writing.
  - Have students reflect on the impact and punctuation of the nonrestrictive elements they added.

Figure 3.6 depicts this instructional process in an easy-to-follow flowchart.

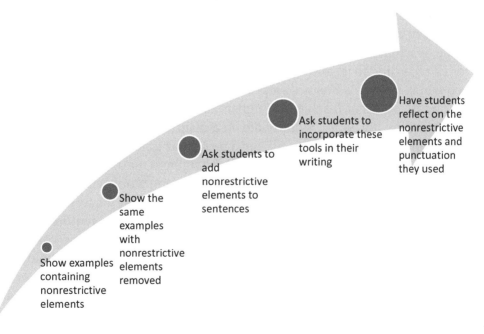

Figure 3.6 Punctuating Nonrestrictive Elements Instructional Flowchart.

4

Maintaining Consistency in Style and Tone

What Does It Mean to Maintain Consistency in Style and Tone?

Common Core Language Standard 6.3 calls for students to "Maintain consistency in style and tone" when writing (Common Core State Standards Initiative, 2010). Let us begin our discussion of this standard by first addressing what is meant by the "style and tone" of a piece of writing. The National Council of Teachers of English (NCTE) statement on Professional Knowledge of the Teaching of Writing sheds light on this topic, explaining that writing varies according to its audience and purpose and pointing out that "a note to a cousin is not like a business report, which is different again from a poem" (National Council of Teachers of English, 2016). Each of these pieces of writing mentioned by the NCTE would take on a distinct style and tone. The author of a business report would decide on a particular tone then would make specific stylistic choices, such as the kind of language used, to create this tone. Similarly, when writing a note to one's cousin, one would think about what kind of tone the note should have and use language that fits this tone.

It is important to note that this Common Core Standard requires our students to not only understand what the style and tone of a piece of writing is, but also to "maintain consistency" with it. In order for our students to do this, they must keep the desired tone of a piece of writing in mind the entire time they are creating it and make sure that the stylistic choices they make align with that tone. For example, a student writing an informational report on the Revolutionary War in an objective tone would want to keep that same tone throughout the piece. If the student began the piece in a formal tone

Element	Description
1. Style and tone	The language used in a piece of writing must align with the piece's audience and purpose. A letter to a possible employer would have a different tone (and use different kinds of language) than a note to a friend.
2. Consistency	Once a writer decides on an appropriate style and tone for a piece of writing, that tone must be used consistently throughout. If a piece begins in an informal way, the reader would be confused if it then shifted to a formal tone.

Figure 4.1 Key Elements of Maintaining Consistency in Style and Tone.

and halfway through it started using informal language and slang terms, the reader would probably be confused and distracted. Figure 4.1 outlines the main components of this standard: that students select a style and tone that is appropriate for a piece of writing and that they keep that tone consistent throughout the piece.

Why Maintaining Consistency in Style and Tone Is Important to Good Writing

Maintaining consistency in style and tone is an important element of effective writing for two reasons: (1) it allows for the entire piece of writing to align with the piece's audience and purpose; and (2) it eliminates the confusion that would come with an unexpected shift in tone. Let us look at each of these reasons in more detail, examining some published texts that illustrate each of these ideas.

First, let us explore how maintaining consistency in style and tone allows for an entire piece of writing to align with its audience and purpose. We know from the NCTE statement on Professional Knowledge of the Teaching of Writing previously addressed in this chapter that authors vary the styles and tones of their works based on the intended readers and the purposes of those works. Once authors select the appropriate tones for pieces they create, they must remember to apply those tones consistently. For example, in Lemony Snicket's (1999) book *The Bad Beginning* (the first of the series of *Unfortunate Events* books), the author creates an ominous tone designed to align with the misfortunes that befall the book's main characters, the Baudelaire orphans, and meet the expectations of readers who want an eerie story. The book's opening lines capture this tone:

> If you are interested in stories with happy endings, you would be better off reading some other book. In this book, not only is there no happy ending, there is no happy beginning and very few happy things happen in the middle.
>
> (p. 1)

Because this book begins with such a specific tone, its effectiveness depends in part on the author consistently applying it. If, as the book continues, the author no longer uses the foreboding tone that characterizes the text's opening lines, the book would not be as effective. Its tone would no longer align with the orphans' unpleasant experiences and its distinctive nature would be lost, disappointing readers who expect this style of narration. Fortunately, this is not the case, as this book maintains its ominous tone. A sentence that appears later in the text reads, "For instance, people who hate stories in which terrible things happen to small children should put this book down immediately" (p. 84). By consistently applying this distinctive style and tone, Lemony Snicket ensures *The Bad Beginning* achieves the same effect on its readers throughout.

Now, let us investigate the way that maintaining consistency in style and tone eliminates the confusion that would come with unexpected shifts in these elements. Nikki Grimes' (2002) novel *Bronx Masquerade* describes the experiences of a group of students who learn about themselves and others by writing poetry. While we hear from a number of characters in the novel, a young man named Tyrone emerges consistently throughout the book, commenting on issues raised in his classmates' poems. Tyrone speaks in an informal style and tone that reveals his distinct personality. For example, early in the novel (before the students begin sharing their poems) Tyrone comments on the lack of hope he has for his future, saying, "Future? What I got is right here, right now, spending time with my homeys. Wish there was some future to talk about. I could use me some future" (p. 8). One reason that Tyrone's comments are effective is that he maintains this same style and tone throughout the book. If his tone changed between the informal style exhibited here and formal language with no explanation of the reason for this change, readers may become confused and distracted by this inconsistency. For example, if Tyrone's statement about his future was then followed by a very formal statement, readers might focus more on trying to determine the reason for this change in tone than on the message of Tyrone's comments. By using a consistent style and tone when crafting Tyrone's comments, Nikki Grimes avoids unnecessary distraction and illustrates the importance of this grammatical concept. In the next section, we will take a look inside a sixth-grade classroom and observe a group of students working on the importance of style and tone to effective writing.

A Classroom Snapshot

As part of an interdisciplinary unit with their social studies class, my sixth graders have just begun reading Mary Kay Phelan's (1976) nonfiction book, *The Story of the Boston Massacre*, in English class. One of the reasons I am excited about this project is that I see this as an excellent opportunity to further help my students understand the importance of writers maintaining consistency in style and tone.

In the past two classes, my students and I have been discussing what it means to maintain consistency in style and tone. We have discussed what this standard means and why it is important to effective writing, and I have shown them the Lemony Snicket and Nikki Grimes examples described in the previous section to illustrate what specific styles and tones can look like. We have discussed how those pieces would be weakened if their respective authors stopped utilizing the specific tones they feature.

I open the lesson by praising their recent efforts: "You've been doing such a great job talking about maintaining consistency in style and tone. You did great work when we discussed the tones in *The Bad Beginning* and in *Bronx Masquerade*. Today, we're going to take our work with this to another level. Please take out your copies of *The Story of the Boston Massacre* and I'll explain what we'll do today."

I tell the students that this book, like the others we examined, has a certain style and tone to it and remind them that it is important that authors use this tone consistently so that the book makes sense and does not confuse the reader. Since the students have just started working with the book, I connect it to the grammatical concept at hand by asking them, "What do you notice about the style and tone of the book so far?"

I smile when I see many students raise their hands; I call on a young lady who states, "It doesn't sound like the guy in *Bronx Masquerade*. He used casual and slang words. This isn't like that."

"That's a great point," I reply. "The character of Tyrone in *Bronx Masquerade* uses an informal tone. The tone here is more formal."

After other students respond with similar insights, I continue. "You made some very good comments there about the formal tone of this text. Now, here are the directions for your next activity: I'd like you to work with a partner and find a sentence from the first chapter that you think is written in an especially formal tone. There are a lot of lines written in this way; you only need to find one. Once you've found it, write it down."

The students look through the text and I circulate, noticing the sentences that they are finding. They seem to have no problem finding sections from the text that are written in formal language, which assures me that they are indeed comfortable identifying this style and tone. I sit down with one pair of students who tell me that they have identified the sentence "Hatred of these officials has become widespread" in the book. When I ask them why they picked out this sentence, one student explains, "It tells us that the people in Boston hated the British officials, but it's formal. It doesn't use expressions or slang or sound like someone's talking casually to a friend."

Once it seems like the students have all identified these sentences, I give them the next set of directions: "Good job finding those sentences," I say, calling them to attention. Now, it's time for the next part of the activity. Take that original formal sentence and translate it into one that's written informally. You're going to take this sentence and make it sound like one that doesn't fit with the style and tone of the text. It won't sound formal anymore; instead, it will have an informal tone. You can change it to use expressions, abbreviations, or other things that you think will make it sound less formal. I'll come around and answer any questions you have. After you do this, I'm going to ask you to share with the class the original, formal sentences and the new, informal version you came up with.

The students get to work on this next component, taking the original formal sentences that they identified and turning them into informal ones. They seem to be having fun with this, as some groups are smiling about the sharp contrasts in tone between the original works and the ones they have created. I again move around the room, checking in with pairs of students as they work to complete the activity. After some time has passed, I call the class together and ask for volunteers to share the original sentence and the new, informal one they created. One of the first groups to share is the one that selected "Hatred of these officials has become widespread" from the text. After one of the group members reads this original sentence aloud, the other shares the revised version: "Man, people can't stand those guys!"

Students in the class smile and laugh, as do I. "That's great," I tell them. "You did a nice job of changing that sentence from its original formal tone to a much more casual one." I ask for other volunteers and a number of hands go up. I call on a group that shares the sentence "The news brought great rejoicing in Boston." After they read this sentence, I ask them to tell the class what they changed it to.

"We changed it to 'People in Boston were fired up!'" one student in the group shared.

"Very good," I reply. "That's definitely a different tone."

Recommendations for Teaching Students to Maintain Consistency in Style and Tone

In this section, I describe a step-by-step instructional process to use when teaching students to maintain consistency in the style and tone they use when writing. The instructional steps I recommend are: (1) show students published examples of different styles and tones and explain how authors create specific tones in their works; (2) ask students to change the styles and tones in published works; (3) discuss with students how the revised pieces compare to the original works; and (4) have students focus on maintaining consistent styles and tones in their own writings. Before beginning this instructional process, I recommend using the information at the beginning of this chapter (such as the terms defined in Figure 4.1) to ensure students understand what "style" and "tone" mean in this context and how these terms are related to consistency. Once you have laid this foundation, then you can help your students apply these ideas and understand why they are important to good writing using the process described here.

1. Show Students Published Examples of Different Styles and Tones and Explain How Authors Create Specific Tones in Their Works

The first step in this instructional process is to show students published works that represent a range of styles and tones, and talk with them about what the authors of those works do to create these specific tones. Providing students with a range of styles and tones allows them to see the variety of ways authors use this concept in their works and illustrates some of the many possibilities for crafting a tone in a piece of writing. For example, you could show students excerpts from each of the three published works referenced in this chapter: Lemony Snicket's *The Bad Beginning*, Nikki Grimes' *Bronx Masquerade*, and Mary Kay Phelan's *The Story of the Boston Massacre*. After you show students these excerpts, talk with them about what kind of tone each one has and how each author achieves this specific tone. Doing so can help students understand that the specific tones authors create in their works are intentional and are achieved through particular decisions they make in their writing—an author interested in creating a formal tone will choose one kind of language, while an author looking to create an informal tone will use different language. One practice that has been helpful for me involves showing my students a graphic organizer that contains published examples from literature, identifies the specific tone each example has, and explains how the author achieved this tone.

Figure 4.2 contains examples from *The Bad Beginning*, *Bronx Masquerade*, and *The Story of the Boston Massacre*, identifies the kind of tone each piece has, and explains how the author creates this tone.

Title and Author of Text	Excerpt	Tone in this Excerpt	How the Author Creates this Tone
The Bad Beginning by Lemony Snicket	"If you are interested in stories with happy endings, you would be better off reading some other book. In this book, not only is there no happy ending, there is no happy beginning and very few happy things happen in the middle" (p. 1).	Ominous	The author creates an ominous tone (in other words, one that suggests negative things will happen) by repeating that happy things do not take place in this book.
Bronx Masquerade by Nikki Grimes	"Future? What I got is right here, right now, spending time with my homeys. Wish there was some future to talk about. I could use me some future" (p. 8).	Casual	The casual tone here comes from slang terms such as "homeys" and examples of informal dialect such as "What I got" (instead of the more formal "What I have").
The Story of the Boston Massacre by Mary Kay Phelan	"The law-making body is composed of two houses: the Council, or upper house, and the Assembly, or lower house" (p. 15).	Formal	The author of this piece creates a formal tone by discussing the subject matter in a factual way, using academic language, and refraining from using any emotion in this description.

Figure 4.2 Published Texts and Their Tones.

2. Ask Students to Change the Styles and Tones in Published Works

The next step in this process is to ask students to select excerpts from published pieces and change their styles and tones. This chapter's classroom snapshot section describes one way this activity can look in action. In this particular instance, the students used a nonfiction text written in a formal, objective tone, selected specific sentences, and changed their tones by making them much more casual. I recommend having all students work with the same text when doing this activity because everyone will then understand the tone of the original work (and therefore understand how the new tone in the altered piece is different from the original one). This activity requires students to understand what the tone of the original piece is, how the author achieved it, and what the author would need to do to create a different kind of tone. For example, in the classroom snapshot, I refer to a conversation with a student who notes that the sentence "Hatred of these officials has become widespread" (Phelan, 1976, p. 2) is formal, explaining that "It doesn't use expressions or slang or sound like someone's talking casually to a friend." This activity can be done with writing that employs any style or tone; the key aspects are that the students can identify the tone in which the author originally wrote the piece, select a line that represents that tone, and finally change the selected line to a different kind of tone.

3. Discuss with Students How the Revised Pieces Compare to the Original Works

After students have changed the tones in published excerpts, the next step is to talk with them about how the new pieces compare to the original works. To do this, I recommend giving each student (or group of students if they

Original Text	The Text's Tone	How the Author Created this Tone	Your Revised Version of this Text	The Text's Tone	How You Created this Tone

Figure 4.3 Tone Comparison Chart.

worked collaboratively on the activity) the chart depicted in Figure 4.3 (and included in reproducible form in the appendix). This chart asks the students to write the original text, the new version they came up with, the tone of each, and how the author of each piece created that tone.

When students fill out this chart, they are challenged to not only reflect on the tone of each text, but also how the author of each piece created this tone. I have found that my students often benefit from seeing an example of a chart such as this before filling one out, so I like to show them a model "Tone Comparison Chart" that I have filled out before asking them to create their own. Figure 4.4 contains a model of this chart that I have shown

Original Text	The Text's Tone	How the Author Created this Tone	Your Revised Version of this Tone	The Text's Tone	How You Created this Tone
"Future? What I got is right here, right now, spending time with my homeys. Wish there was some future to talk about. I could use me some future" (p. 8).	Casual	The casual tone here comes from slang terms such as "homeys" and examples of informal dialect such as "What I got" (instead of the more formal "What I have").	Future? What I have is the ability to spend time right now with my friends. I wish there was a future to talk about. I could definitely benefit from a future.	Formal	This version's formal tone comes from eliminating the informal language, such as "homeys" and "got" in the original version, and replacing it with more formal language. For example, I replaced "homeys" with friends" and changed "What I got" to "What I have."

Figure 4.4 Model Tone Comparison Chart.

students so that they have a clear understanding of what to do in this activity. This version uses the excerpt from *Bronx Masquerade* depicted in Figure 4.2 and adds to it by also including a revised version of that excerpt and an analysis of it.

After you show students a model such as this one and ask them to complete their own version using the text they used, it is time to ask them to share their ideas. I always find it especially interesting to hear the students describe how the author created the original piece's tone and then compare it with the way they created the tone in the revised versions they made. For example, recall the group in the classroom snapshot that changed the sentence "The news brought great rejoicing in Boston" to "People in Boston were fired up!" When, in a follow-up lesson, I asked this group to identify the tone of the new piece and explain how they created it, one of the group's members explained,

> The new version is much more casual. We made it this way by using the expression "fired up" instead of saying "great rejoicing" like in the way it was (originally). "Fired up" sounds more like something you'd say to a friend. The way the author wrote is a lot more formal.

This student's comments show a strong understanding of the way these linguistic choices result in the pieces of writing in which they are found having different tones.

4. Have Students Focus on Maintaining Consistent Styles and Tones in Their Own Writings

The final step in this instructional process is to ask students to turn their attention to their own pieces of writing, focusing specifically on the consistency in style and tone in those works. To do this, ask students to take out any piece of writing they are currently working on, no matter what genre it is. Once students have written work to examine, ask them to read their work carefully, paying attention to the following reflection questions:

1. What is the intended tone of this piece?
2. What language did I use to create this tone?
3. Are there any sections in this piece that do not align with that tone? How?
4. If so, how can I change those sections to make sure that they align with the intended tone?

I recommend posting these questions in a prominently displayed location so that students can easily keep them in mind as they review their pieces. As the students examine their pieces with style and tone in mind, I ask them to answer each of these questions in their notebooks so that I know that they have taken the time to carefully reflect on them. After I have given the students enough time to consider these questions, I hold individual writing conferences with each of them, focusing specifically on the tone in the student's piece, how the student creates that tone, and if there are any sections that should be revised to align with this tone.

Final Thoughts on Maintaining Consistency in Style and Tone

- Common Core Language Standard 6.3 calls for students to "Maintain consistency in style and tone" when writing.
- The style and tone of a piece of writing varies according to its audience and purpose (National Council of Teachers of English, 2016).
- The NCTE (2016) points out that "a note to a cousin is not like a business report, which is different again from a poem." Each of these pieces would have a distinct style and tone.
- In order for students to maintain consistency in the style and tone of their writing, they must keep the desired tone of a piece of writing in mind the entire time that they are creating it and make sure that the stylistic choices they make align with that tone.
- Maintaining consistency in style and tone is an important element of effective writing for two reasons:
  1. It allows for the entire piece of writing to align with its audience and purpose.
  2. It eliminates the confusion that would come with an unexpected shift in tone.
- When teaching students to maintain consistency in style and tone:
  - Show students published examples of different styles and tones and explain how authors create specific tones in their works.
  - Ask students to change the styles and tones in published works.
  - Discuss with students how the revised pieces compare to the original works.
  - Have students focus on maintaining consistent styles and tones in their own writings.

Figure 4.5 depicts this instructional process in an easy-to-follow flowchart.

Maintaining Consistency in Style and Tone ◆ 59

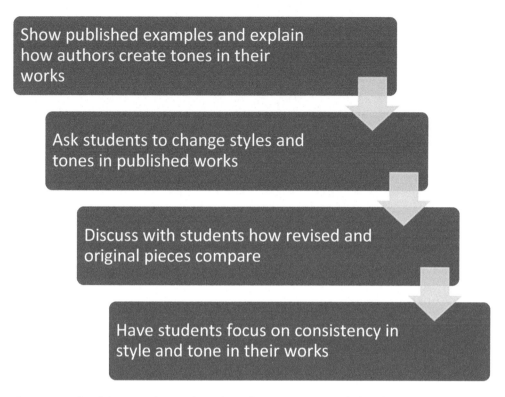

Figure 4.5 Maintaining Consistency in Style and Tone Instructional Flowchart.

Part II

Grammatical Concepts Aligned with Grade 7 Common Core Language Standards

Introduction

In Part I, we looked at key grammatical concepts aligned with Grade 6 Common Core Language Standards. Now, we'll examine four important grammatical concepts reflected in the Common Core Language Standards for Grade 7. First, in Chapter 5, we'll consider the concept of using simple, compound, complex, and compound-complex sentences. Next, in Chapter 6, we'll reflect on the importance of using phrases and clauses to add detail to writing while also recognizing and correcting dangling modifiers. After that, in Chapter 7, we'll look closely at the idea of choosing language that expresses ideas precisely and eliminates wordiness and redundancy. The section concludes with Chapter 8, in which we'll examine the importance of distinguishing among the connotations of words with similar denotations. Consistent with the chapters in Part I, each chapter will begin with information about the concept's features and a discussion of its importance to effective writing. The chapter will then transition to a classroom Snapshot that describes my experiences teaching the focal strategy to a seventh-grade English class. After that, I'll share recommendations to keep in mind while teaching your students about the chapter's topic before concluding with some final thoughts on the concept's importance and instructional strategies related to it.

While they vary in their specific attributes, the concepts featured in this section are all important tools to effective writing that authors can use to enhance their works. The simple, compound, complex, and compound-complex sentences described in Chapter 5 are tactics that authors strategically use to provide varying levels of detail to particular statements. As we'll see in that chapter, all of these sentence types are useful to strong writing as long they're used with clear understandings of the benefits and features of each type. The phrases and clauses discussed in Chapter 6 are useful for enhancing writing with additional detail that helps the reader envision what the writer is describing. The examples in this chapter will convey the importance of detail-oriented grammatical concepts such as relative clauses and participial phrases, while also providing ideas on using these concepts in clear ways that avoid potential confusion. The next concept discussed in this section, using language that expresses ideas clearly while eliminating unnecessary wordiness, focuses on specific nouns and strong verbs that allow authors to express information clearly without using more words and phrases than necessary. For example, the strong verb "tossed" expresses an action more clearly than the weaker verb "threw" and with better language economy than "threw very gently." The final concept discussed in this section, distinguishing among connotations of words with similar denotations, is a key concept for writers to understand in order to ensure the clarity and effectiveness of their language. As explained in the chapter, "Good writers are aware of the kind of tone they are creating in their writing and are sure that the words they select have connotations that align with that tone." The chapter describes how strong writers keep connotation in mind when selecting words they use in their works, highlighting examples such as "pushy" and "assertive" that have similar denotations but different connotations.

The explanations, examples, and suggestions in these chapters will give you strong insights regarding these important seventh-grade concepts and how to teach your students about their importance. Now, let's get started!

5

Using Simple, Compound, Complex, and Compound-Complex Sentences

What Are Simple, Compound, Complex, and Compound-Complex Sentences?

Common Core Language Standard 7.1 calls for students to "Choose among simple, compound, complex, and compound-complex sentences to signal differing relationships among ideas" as part of a more general statement that students need to "Demonstrate command of the conventions of standard English grammar and usage when writing or speaking" (Common Core State Standards Initiative, 2010). No matter our direct connection to the Common Core, the concept of simple, compound, complex, and compound-complex sentences is an important tool for our students to understand. These sentence types provide variation in writing, as they differ in their structures, effects, and amounts of detail. Let us begin our discussion of this standard by first exploring what simple, compound, complex, and compound-complex sentences are.

Simple Sentences

Simple sentences consist of one independent clause, which is a group of words that contains a subject and verb and expresses a complete thought. For example, the sentence "Kate ran on the treadmill" is a simple sentence because it contains one independent clause. Understanding simple sentences is the starting point for learning about the different sentence types described in this standard. Compound, complex, and compound-complex sentences are all expanded versions of simple sentences. Simple sentences are the only sentences that consist solely of one independent clause; the other three kinds contain one independent clause plus another kind of clause added to it.

Compound Sentences

While simple sentences consist of only one independent clause, compound sentences consist of two or more independent clauses joined together. There are two ways the independent clauses in compound sentences are linked: (1) by a comma and coordinating conjunction; and (2) by a semicolon. Let us examine each of these types of compound sentences.

Compound Sentences Containing a Comma and Coordinating Conjunction

Many compound sentences use the combination of a comma and a coordinating conjunction to link independent clauses. The coordinating conjunctions are *for*, *and*, *not*, *but*, *or*, *yet*, and *so*. For example, the compound sentence "Kate ran on the treadmill, but Rachel ran on the track" includes two independent clauses ("Kate ran on the treadmill" and "Rachel ran on the track"), which are linked by the coordinating conjunction "but" and a comma.

Compound Sentences Containing a Semicolon

Some compound sentences use a semicolon to link two independent clauses instead of the combination of a comma and coordinating conjunction. If we revised the sentence "Kate ran on the treadmill, but Rachel ran on the track" to create a compound sentence featuring a semicolon, we would have "Kate ran on the treadmill; Rachel ran on the track." Writers sometimes elect to use semicolons when linking independent clauses because semicolons can make compound sentences as direct and concise as possible.

Complex Sentences

Complex sentences contain an independent clause and at least one dependent clause. A dependent clause is a group of words that contains a subject and verb but cannot stand on its own as a sentence (in contrast to an independent clause, which contains a subject and verb and can stand on its own). For example, the clause "while she trained for the race" is an example of a dependent clause; it contains a subject and a verb but cannot stand on its own as a sentence. A clause such as this would be used in a complex sentence to provide additional information about the action described in an independent clause. If we combine this dependent clause with the previously used independent clause "Kate ran on the treadmill," we have the complex sentence "While she trained for the race, Kate ran on the treadmill."

Compound-Complex Sentences

Compound-complex sentences contain at least two independent clauses and at least one dependent clause. Thus far in this chapter, we have looked at the dependent clause "while she trained for the race" and the independent clauses "Kate ran on the treadmill" and "Rachel ran on the track." If we revise the dependent clause to contain the plural pronoun "they" instead of the singular "she," we can combine all of these clauses to create the compound-complex sentence "While they trained for the race, Kate ran on the treadmill, but Rachel ran on the track." Compound-complex sentences combine the extra description offered by dependent clauses with at least two independent clauses.

Figures 5.1, 5.2, 5.3, and 5.4 illustrate major points related to simple, compound, complex, and compound-complex sentences.

Grammatical Concept	Simple Sentence
What is a simple sentence?	A simple sentence consists of one independent clause.
What is an example of a simple sentence?	Kate ran on the treadmill.
Why is this an example of a simple sentence?	It contains one independent clause and no dependent clauses.

Figure 5.1 Simple Sentence.

Grammatical Concept	Compound Sentence
What is a compound sentence?	A compound sentence consists of two or more independent clauses joined together by either: (1) a comma and coordinating conjunction; or (2) a semicolon.
What are some examples of compound sentences?	1. Kate ran on the treadmill, but Rachel ran on the track. 2. Kate ran on the treadmill; Rachel ran on the track.
Why are these examples of compound sentences?	• Each sentence contains two independent clauses. • In example one, the two independent clauses are joined by the coordinating conjunction "but." • In example two, the two independent clauses are joined by a semicolon.

Figure 5.2 Compound Sentence.

Grammatical Concept	Complex Sentence
What is a complex sentence?	A complex sentence consists of an independent clause and at least one dependent clause.
What is an example of a complex sentence?	While she trained for the race, Kate ran on the treadmill.
Why is this an example of a complex sentence?	It contains a dependent clause ("While she trained for the race") and an independent clause ("Kate ran on the treadmill").

Figure 5.3 Complex Sentence.

Grammatical Concept	Compound-Complex Sentence
What is a compound-complex sentence?	A compound-complex sentence consists of at least two independent clauses and at least one dependent clause.
What is an example of a compound-complex sentence?	While they trained for the race, Kate ran on the treadmill, but Rachel ran on the track.
Why is this an example of a compound-complex sentence?	It contains a dependent clause ("While they trained for the race") and two independent clauses ("Kate ran on the treadmill" and "Rachel ran on the track").

Figure 5.4 Compound-Complex Sentence.

Why Simple, Compound, Complex, and Compound-Complex Sentences Are Important to Good Writing

Simple, compound, complex, and compound-complex sentences are important tools that writers use to provide additional levels of details to particular statements. Effective writers use each of these sentences purposefully, with a clear understanding of the benefits of each: a writer would use a simple sentence to make a point clearly and concisely, a compound sentence to combine multiple statements, a complex sentence to provide additional detail regarding the context of a particular statement, and a compound-complex sentence to provide contextual details while also linking multiple statements together. In this section, we will take a look at published examples of each of these sentence types and explore the benefits of using each sentence type in its particular situation.

A simple sentence in George Takei's (2019) graphic memoir *They Called Us Enemy* illustrates the way authors use these kinds of sentences to make direct and concise statements. This book describes the experiences of and discrimination faced by Takei, his family, and other Japanese Americans during the Japanese Internment. When Takei writes "My parents met in California" (p. 11), he provides readers with a clear and straightforward statement about his parents and family. While Takei could have linked the statement with other clauses, he chose to keep the sentence focused on this specific statement by using this simple sentence.

At another point in *They Called Us Enemy*, Takei uses a compound sentence to link two independent clauses that contain related ideas. In the context of a discussion of his parents having their first baby (which was George Takei himself) and the ways parenthood changed their lives, Takei writes of his parents "He would call her Mama from then on, and she would call him Daddy" (p. 12). This compound sentence contains two independent clauses—"he would call her Mama from then on" and "she would call him Daddy"—linked by a comma and the coordinating conjunction "and." While Takei could have written them as separate sentences, his decision to link them in a compound sentence impacts the writing in two ways: (1) it shows that the ideas in each of these independent clauses are related to one another; and (2) it allows for the text to read more smoothly by avoiding the short, choppy sentences that would be created if these two statements were not linked. If Takei had written these as separate sentences, they would read, "He would call her Mama from then on. She would call him Daddy," instead of the more cohesive and smoothly written way it currently appears.

Now, let us take a look at a complex sentence George Takei uses in *They Called Us Enemy*. The sentence "Whenever we would approach a town, we were forced to draw the shade" (p. 40), which describes how Japanese Americans who were made to travel by train to government-run facilities were also forced to pull down the train's window shades when passing through populated areas, contains both an independent clause ("we were forced to draw the shade") as well as a dependent clause ("whenever we would approach a town"). The dependent clause in this sentence adds important contextual information, as it lets readers know the situation when the independent clause took place. While this sentence could simply read, "We were forced to draw the shade," the dependent clause lets readers know that this took place when the trains entered towns and could be seen by many people. Takei's use of a complex sentence here provides readers with important contextual information that they would not otherwise have.

Finally, let us examine an example from literature of a compound-complex sentence in *They Called Us Enemy*, which George Takei uses when describing the actions of Herbert Nicholson, a Quaker missionary who brought books and other forms of assistance to Japanese Americans imprisoned in internment camps (in this sentence, an internment camp called Manzanar). In the sentence "After he was attacked, the people of Manzanar assumed they'd seen the last of Herbert … but sure enough, the next month on that same date, Herbert was back at Manzanar with more books" (pp. 146–147), Takei uses the dependent clause "after he was attacked" in conjunction with the independent clauses "the people of Manzanar assumed they'd seen the last of Herbert" and "the next month on that same date, Herbert was back at Manzanar with more books." The use of this compound-complex sentence allows Takei to link two independent but related statements, while also providing detail related to the important context surrounding this event (specifically, the fact that Herbert Nicholson was attacked for trying to help Japanese Americans). If Takei chose not to use a compound-complex sentence here, this sentence would not convey the full details of the situation. Eliminating the dependent clause would take the context of the situation away, and eliminating one of the independent clauses would result in the sentence no longer expressing these two related statements. Only through the use of this compound-complex sentence can George Takei fully combine and reveal the information conveyed in this sentence.

So, why are simple, compound, complex, and compound-complex sentences important to good writing? As these examples illustrate, each one of these sentence types is a tool an author can use to express a particular statement. No sentence type is inherently better than another, just as no tool is better than another. Rather, each is most effective when used in a situation that calls for it. The best writing will use a combination of these sentence types, with each one used in the way that best aligns with its features. Now, let us look inside a seventh-grade classroom and observe some middle schoolers working on the benefits of each of these sentence types.

 ## A Classroom Snapshot

A class of seventh graders and I are working on simple, compound, complex, and compound-complex sentences. Today's lesson focuses on discussing the strengths of each sentence type by comparing each to a specific tool used for a particular purpose. My goal for this lesson is to deepen the students' understandings of simple, compound, complex, and compound-complex sentences by moving them beyond a basic understanding of what these sentence types are and towards an awareness of why writers use them.

When the students enter the room, they see that I have posted four pieces of chart paper on the board, each containing one of the sentences featured in the charts in Figures 5.1, 5.2, 5.3, and 5.4. One piece of paper says "Simple Sentence: Kate ran on the treadmill"; another says "Compound Sentence: Kate ran on the treadmill, but Rachel ran on the track"; yet another says "Complex Sentence: While she trained for the race, Kate ran on the treadmill"; and the final piece of paper reads "Compound-Complex Sentence: While they trained for the race, Kate ran on the treadmill, but Rachel ran on the track."

I begin this activity by reminding students that they have seen these sentences already: "These are the sentences we looked at in our last class when we discussed what simple, compound, complex, and compound-complex sentences are." Many of the students nod. "Now that we know those fundamentals, today we're going to think of these sentences a little differently. Since you know what each one of these sentences is, today I'm going to ask you to really think like writers. I'm going to ask you *why* writers would use these sentences."

I continue to explain to the students that I will divide them into four groups. I then say that each group is going to take one sentence type and answer this question: "Why would a writer choose to use this sentence type?"

"In order to answer this question," I explain, "you'll need to think about the benefits of your sentence type. What are the benefits of using a simple sentence? A compound one? Any of the others? If you can describe some benefits of using your group's type of sentence, then you can express why a writer would use it."

I tell them that group one will take simple sentences, group two will work on compound sentences, group three will take complex sentences, and group four will work on compound-complex sentences. I divide the students into groups and tell them that I will move around the room and listen to their ideas as they work, explaining that after each group formulates its ideas, all of the groups will share their thoughts with the class.

Once the students are in groups and discussing the reasons why a writer would choose to use their assigned sentence type, I begin to check in with the groups by listening to them as they formulate their ideas. I first sit down with the group working on simple sentences and am pleased with what I hear. "Simple sentences are real clear," explains one student to his group members. "A benefit of them is they make their point really clearly. There's no distraction."

After praising this student for her response, I move around the room some more, next checking in with the group working on complex sentences. Sitting down with this group, I ask the students to share some benefits that they believe complex sentences possess. "They have dependent clauses," answers one student.

"That's true," I reply. "That's certainly a fact about complex sentences. But why is that a *benefit*?"

"Because," responds another student in the group, "dependent clauses give you more detail, like when or why something happened."

"Great! Look at that sentence on the chart," I say, directing the students to the front of the room and the complex sentence that reads, "While she trained for the race, Kate ran on the treadmill." "What's a benefit of the dependent clause there?" I ask.

"It gives detail," answers the student. "It says when she ran on the treadmill."

I compliment this student's insight into the benefits of this sentence type and continue to circulate the room, checking in with the other groups. Once I have done that, I address the class and explain that each group will share its thoughts about why a writer would choose to use this sentence type. "Let us know your thoughts," I explain, "about why writers would use your sentence. In other words, what benefits does your sentence have?"

Before the students share, I write each sentence type on the board and explain what I will do while the students present: "When you share your thoughts, I'll write the main points of what you say on the board here next to your sentence type. That way, everyone can see your comments up on the board."

Each group shares and I record highlights of their responses on the board, which are illustrated in Figure 5.5.

After the students have shared these thoughts, I praise their insights: "Great job today. This is an outstanding start to thinking about the benefits of each of these sentence types."

Recommendations for Teaching Students about Simple, Compound, Complex, and Compound-Complex Sentences

In this section, I describe a step-by-step instructional process to use when teaching students about simple, compound, complex, and compound-complex

Sentence Type	Benefits Observed by Students
Simple	Make points very clearly.
Compound	Connect different statements in one sentence.
Complex	Use dependent clauses to give detail about something happening.
Compound-Complex	Give extra detail with dependent clauses while also combining different statements.

Figure 5.5 Sentence Types and Benefits Observed by Students.

sentences. The instructional steps I recommend are: (1) help students discuss the benefits of each sentence type; (2) ask students to try to find these sentence types in literature; (3) have students analyze an author's use of a particular sentence type; and (4) ask students to use each of the sentence types purposefully in their own writing. Since this instructional process is designed to help students apply their understandings of simple, compound, complex, and compound-complex sentences, I recommend using the information at the beginning of this chapter, such as the examples and definitions in Figures 5.1, 5.2, 5.3, and 5.4, to ensure that students understand the fundamentals of these sentence types before beginning these instructional activities.

1. Help Students Discuss the Benefits of Each Sentence Type

The first step in this instructional process is to help students discuss the benefits of each of these four sentence types. Focusing on these benefits can help students understand how simple, compound, complex, and compound-complex sentences are tools that writers use purposefully in their works. If students are aware that simple sentences, for example, are beneficial because they allow readers to make statements in a direct and straightforward way, they can understand why writers might choose to use these sentences in some contexts, while electing to use other sentence types in different situations.

To help students discuss these benefits, I recommend engaging them in an activity such as the one described in the classroom snapshot section. Once you have explained to the students the key elements of these sentence types and shown them examples of each, ask them to work together and explain why an author might choose to use each sentence type and the benefits of using that kind of sentence. As I did in the lesson described in the classroom snapshot, I recommend dividing the students into groups in order to complete this task. Since the students will be beginning to explore this concept, they can benefit from bouncing ideas off of one another and engaging in what Barnes (1992) calls exploratory talk: conversations about a new and challenging topic that help students formulate ideas.

When my seventh graders worked together on this topic, they began to see these sentence types as not just things to memorize, but tools that are important to effective writing. Recall, for example, the student who initially told me that a benefit of complex sentences is that they have dependent clauses. I responded to this student by saying that this was a true statement, but also pushed her thinking to another level by asking *why* this is a benefit. Considering the benefits of this sentence type allowed this student and the others in the class to look at these concepts as tools that writers purposefully use, rather than facts to memorize and then forget.

2. Ask Students to Try to Find These Sentence Types in Literature

The next step in this instructional process is to ask to students to try to find examples of these sentence types in literature. Making this direct connection to literature further illustrates the importance of these sentence types to effective writing, as students are able to see how published writers use these grammatical concepts authentically. This can be done with the students' independent reading books or with a text the entire the class is reading together. As students find different sentence types in literature, they will become more familiar with them and further understand their importance to effective writing. Since not every book on every student's reading level will have all four of these sentence types, I recommend not requiring that students find all four sentence types. I suggest giving the students a certain amount of time (I will often give 15 minutes) and asking them to see which of these sentence types they can find, reminding them that they are not required to find all of them, and instructing them to write down an example of each type they locate. I tell my students that since authors only use these sentence types when necessary, some texts will not need to include all of these sentence types, while others will. Asking the students to find what they can rather than mandating that they find all four kinds makes this activity a fun "scavenger hunt" and reduces possible student frustration.

3. Have Students Analyze an Author's Use of a Particular Sentence Type

After students have identified some of these sentence types in literature, I recommend asking them to pick one of the sentences that they found and analyze it in more detail. This analysis calls for each student to do the following: (1) select a sentence that really stood out to them as effective; (2) identify the kind of sentence it is; (3) rewrite the sentence as another sentence type; and (4) explain what would be different if the sentence was written as this other type instead. These analytic steps require the students to move from the concrete (by identifying a type of sentence) to the more complex (by explaining how the revised version of the sentence differs from the original one).

Before I ask students to do this activity, I model it to show them exactly what is expected. Figure 5.6 is a model of this activity using a complex sentence from Jeanne DuPrau's (2003) novel *The City of Ember* that I have used with my students. I will present this chart to students and explain each aspect of it before asking them to fill out a similar chart on their own.

After you show the students this example and discuss it with them, you can then ask your students to complete their own analysis independently. When you ask the students to do this, give them a blank version of the chart

Sentence that Stood Out to You as Effective	Sentence Type	Rewritten as Another Type	What Would be Different if the Sentence Was Written this Way?
"When Lina went to work the next morning, the street was oddly silent" (p. 84).	Complex	The street was oddly silent (simple sentence).	If the sentence was written this way, it would not tell us that the street was silent when Lina went to work. Instead, it would only say that the street was silent. The original version provides more detail and information.

Figure 5.6 Model of Sentence Type Analysis.

in Figure 5.6 to fill out (a blank, reproducible version is available in the appendix). As they work on it, I recommend checking in with them and giving them necessary support, but also making sure that students use their analytic skills.

Figure 5.7 contains a sentence type analysis chart filled out by a student named Erica during this activity. When completing this chart, Erica identified the compound sentence "All of her friends hated lima beans, and she wanted to fit in" in David Shannon's (2004) book *A Bad Case of Stripes*, rewrote it as a simple sentence, and analyzed the differences between those versions.

4. Ask Students to Use Each of the Sentence Types Purposefully in Their Own Writing

The final step of this instructional process is to ask students to use simple, compound, complex, and compound-complex sentences purposefully in their own writing. This step is especially important because it calls for students to use these grammatical concepts in strategic ways to improve the quality of their own works. It is the natural conclusion to this process, which began with students discussing the benefits of these sentence types. Once the students reach the point where they understand these benefits and how published authors use each of these sentence types strategically to maximize those benefits, it is time for them to do the same with their own writing.

Sentence-Type Analysis Chart

Sentence that Stood Out to You as Effective	Sentence Type	Sentence Rewritten as Another Type _Simple_	What Would be Different if the Sentence was Written this Way?
"All of her friends hated lima beans, and she wanted to fit in."	Compound	All her friends hated lima beans	The simple one is just plain. The compound one is longer and exciting.

Figure 5.7 Sentence Type Analysis Chart.

I recommend working on this step with your students by meeting with each of them individually and asking them to first show you an example of each of these four sentence types in their writing and then to explain why they chose to use each particular sentence type in each situation. When I talk with my students about this topic, I listen carefully to their explanations of why they used different sentence types in different situations and challenge them to explain their choices as clearly as possible. I want to make sure my students understand the benefits of each of these sentence types so they can purposefully use simple, compound, complex, and compound-complex sentences to enhance their own works.

Final Thoughts on Simple, Compound, Complex, and Compound-Complex Sentences

- ◆ Simple, compound, complex, and compound-complex sentences are included in Common Core Language Standard 7.1:
  - A simple sentence consists of one independent clause.
  - A compound sentence consists of two or more independent clauses joined together by either: (1) a comma and coordinating conjunction; or (2) a semicolon.

- A complex sentence consists of an independent clause and at least one dependent clause.
- A compound-complex sentence consists of at least two independent clauses and at least one dependent clause.
◆ Effective writers use each of these sentences purposefully, with a clear understanding of the benefits of each. Specifically, a writer would use:
- A simple sentence to make a point clearly and concisely.
- A compound sentence to combine multiple statements.
- A complex sentence to provide additional detail regarding the context of a particular statement.
- A compound-complex sentence to provide contextual details while also linking multiple statements together.
◆ When teaching students about simple, compound, complex, and compound-complex sentences:
- Help students discuss the benefits of each sentence type.
- Ask students to try to find these sentence types in literature.
- Have students analyze an author's use of a particular sentence type.
- Ask students to use each of the sentence types purposefully in their own writing.

Figure 5.8 depicts this instructional process in an easy-to-follow flowchart.

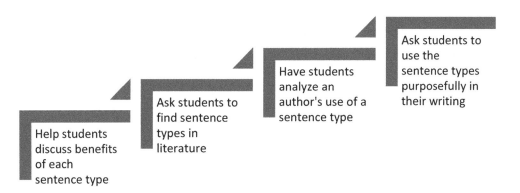

Figure 5.8 Sentence Types Instructional Flowchart.

6

Using Phrases and Clauses while Recognizing and Correcting Dangling Modifiers

What Are Dangling Modifiers?

Common Core Language Standard 7.1 calls for students to "Place phrases and clauses within a sentence, recognizing and correcting dangling modifiers" (Common Core State Standards Initiative, 2010). A modifier is an element of a sentence (such as a word, phrase, or clause) that adds detail. Authors will frequently add modifiers to sentences to provide additional information and allow readers to picture what is taking place. Sounds great, right? Right, except when we are dealing with dangling modifiers. Dangling modifiers are descriptive aspects of sentences that are unclear in what they describe. There are two main ways dangling modifiers manifest themselves in writing: (1) the modifier is not placed next to the noun it is describing; and (2) the noun being described is not included in the sentence at all. Let us take a look at each of these situations.

Modifier Not Placed Next to the Noun It Is Describing

First, let us take a look at a dangling modifier that results from the modifier not being placed next to the noun it is describing. In this situation, the modified noun is in the sentence, but its location makes it seem as if the modifier is actually describing another noun. For example, in the sentence "Worn out from many years of use, my dad took the stereo to the garbage dump," "worn out from many years of use" is a dangling modifier. It is placed next to "my dad," not "the stereo," which is the noun it is likely meant to describe (for the dad's sake, we certainly hope so!). We can correct this sentence by rewriting it as "My dad took the stereo, which was worn out from many years of use, to the garbage dump." If we wanted to retain the original order of the modifier, we could also rewrite the sentence as "Worn out from many years of use, the stereo was taken to the garbage dump by my dad." Either one of these new constructions would eliminate the dangling modifier found in the original version by placing the modifying text next to the noun it is meant to describe.

Noun Being Described Not Included in the Sentence

A dangling modifier can also occur when the noun to which the modifier refers is not included in the sentence. The sentence "Arriving late, the party had already ended" is an example of this; "arriving late" is a dangling modifier because the sentence does not tell us who arrived late. We can eliminate this problem by indicating who arrived late, such as in the sentence "Arriving late, James found that the party had already ended." In this version, the noun being described is included in the sentence and is placed next to the modifier, eliminating any possibility of a dangling modifier. "Arriving late" now clearly modifies James and allows the reader to envision the situation.

Figure 6.1 summarizes the key points and examples regarding dangling modifiers that are discussed in this section.

What Are Some Key Types of Modifiers to Use in Sentences?

In addition to knowing the features of dangling modifiers, it's important to reflect on types of modifiers that authors use to add important details to sentences. For writers to clearly use modifiers in their works, they have to know how to avoid dangling modifiers while also understanding the kinds of tools that they can use to provide important descriptive information. Two especially important modifiers that authors use to add significant details are relative clauses and participial phrases. Let's look at each of these grammatical concepts individually.

Relative Clauses

Relative clauses are modifiers that authors use to describe nouns and pronouns in their works. These clauses typically begin with relative pronouns (*who*, *whose*, *whom*, *which*, and *that*) or relative adverbs (*where*, *when*, and *why*). For example, in the 2017 novel *Refugee*, author Alan Gratz uses two relative clauses in the following sentence, which describes the experiences of a character named Isabel who immigrated to the United States from Cuba, focusing specifically on how she played "The Star-Spangled Banner" salsa-style

Grammatical concept	Dangling Modifiers
What is a dangling modifier?	A dangling modifier is a descriptive element of a sentence that is unclear in what it describes.
How do dangling modifiers appear in writing?	Dangling modifiers appear in two ways: 1. The modifier is not placed next to the noun it is describing. 2. The noun being described is not included in the sentence at all.
What are some examples of dangling modifiers?	1. Worn out from many years of use, my dad took the stereo to the garbage dump. 2. Arriving late, the party had already ended.
Why are these examples of dangling modifiers?	• Number one contains a dangling modifier because the modifier "worn out from many years of use" is not placed next to the noun it is modifying, "the stereo." • Number two contains a dangling modifier because the noun being described is not included in the sentence.
How can these sentences be corrected?	• Number one can be corrected to read, "My dad took the stereo, which was worn out from many years of use, to the garbage dump." • Number two can be corrected to read, "Arriving late, James found out that the party had already ended."

Figure 6.1 Information about Dangling Modifiers.

to honor her family: "She played it salsa for her mother and her father, who had left their homeland, and for her little brother Mariano, who would never know the streets of Havana the way she had" (p. 308). The relative clauses "who had left their homeland" and "who would never know the streets of Havana the way she had" are important modifiers in this sentence: they provide significant information about the individuals being described that increases the level of detail and context in the sentence. By incorporating these relative clauses, Gratz helps readers understand the significance of Isabel's decision and its relevance to her life and family.

Figure 6.2 summarizes some key features and attributes of relative clauses.

What are relative clauses?	Relative clauses are modifiers that describe nouns and pronouns. Relative clauses typically begin with a relative pronoun (*who, whose, whom, which,* and *that*) or a relative adverb (*where, when,* and *why*).
	In some situations, such as in informal communication, the relative pronoun or adverb can be "understood" but not directly stated. For example, one might say "This is the restaurant that I like" or "This is the restaurant I like." In the second version, the relative pronoun "that" is "understood" but not directly stated. For clarity, I recommend using relative pronouns and adverbs to begin relative clauses whenever possible.
Why do writers use them?	Writers use relative clauses to add important identifying and contextual information to their works. Through the use of relative clauses, writing can be much more detailed and informative than if they were not used.
What are some examples?	The players arrived at the stadium *where the championship game will be played.* • In this sentence "where the championship game will be played" is a relative clause describing the stadium. It begins with the relative adverb "where."
	Jane, *who just published her first novel*, is coming to speak to our writing class. • In this sentence, "who just published her first novel" is a relative clause describing Jane. It begins with the relative pronoun "who."

Figure 6.2 Key Components of Relative Clauses.

Participial Phrases

Like relative clauses, participial phrases are modifiers that writers use to provide descriptive information about nouns and pronouns. However, their features are different: instead of beginning with relative pronouns or relative adverbs like relative clauses do, participial phrases begin with present or past participles. The present participle is called the "-ing" form of a verb and the past participle is the "-en" form of a verb. The present participle of a regular verb is formed by adding "-ing" to the base form of the verb; the past participle of a regular verb is formed by adding "-ed" to its base form. (It's important to note, though, that many verbs in the English language are irregular in some ways and therefore deviate from these patterns.)

The 2017 novel *The Epic Fail of Arturo Zamora* by Pablo Cartaya incorporates a number of participial phrases to provide descriptive information. For example, when discussing a situation in which his friend Carmen told an embarrassing story, narrator and protagonist Arturo Zamora uses the participial phrase "wishing she didn't have such a good memory" in the sentence "'That's right,' I said, wishing she didn't have such a good memory," (p. 16). This phrase enhances the level of information in the sentence by incorporating detail and description about Arturo. A bit later in the novel, Arturo uses a participial phrase to describe his chef mother as she interacts with the diners at the family's restaurant. The statement "My mom walked over to the couple, said hello, and then turned to walk away, smiling uncomfortably as she tried to get Abuela to follow her" (p. 27) ends with the participial phrase "smiling uncomfortably as she tried to get Abuela to follow her." This phrase provides readers with information that helps them visualize and understand the situation. Both of these participial phrase examples convey descriptive details that contribute to the reader's awareness of the situations discussed in the novel.

Figure 6.3 discusses some key features and attributes of participial phrases.

What are participial phrases?	Participial phrases are modifiers that describe nouns or pronouns. A participial phrase begins with a present or past participle.
Why do writers use them?	Writers use participial phrase to enhance the level of detail in their works. When authors use participial phrases, they allow their readers to understand key nouns and pronouns in their writing in more detail and with more clarity than if the participial phrases were not used.
What are some examples?	*Smiling at the fans*, the singer took the stage. • In this sentence, "smiling at the fans" is a participial phrase. It begins with the present participle "smiling." The goalie, *focused on stopping the ball*, stood confidently on the field. • In this sentence, "focused on stopping the ball" is a participial phrase." It begins with the past participle "focused."

Figure 6.3 Key Components of Participial Phrases.

Why Is Recognizing and Correcting Dangling Modifiers Important to Good Writing?

It is important that writers are able to recognize and correct dangling modifiers in their works in order to maximize the clarity of their writing. If a piece of writing contains dangling modifiers, readers will be confused about what the modifiers are actually intended to describe. While the description provided by modifying phrases and clauses can add important information to a piece, these modifiers must be incorporated carefully to achieve their potential benefits. In this section, we will take a look at examples of descriptive language from Jack London's (1906) novel *White Fang* and examine how those descriptions would not have the same clarity if they were presented as dangling modifiers.

In *White Fang*, Jack London uses phrases and clauses to add significant details to the text. In the sentence "The wolf-dogs, clustered on the far side of the fire, snarled and bickered among themselves, but evinced no inclination to stray off in the darkness" (p. 172). London includes the phrase "clustered on the far side of the fire" to provide additional information about the wolf-dogs. Note that this modifier is not "dangling" because we can clearly determine what it describes. Part of this modifier's clarity comes from its placement: note that "clustered on the far side of the fire" is placed next to "the wolf-dogs," which it describes. If this phrase was placed away from "the wolf-dogs," the sentence would likely contain a dangling modifier. For example, if London placed this phrase at the end of the sentence, writing, "The wolf-dogs snarled and bickered among themselves, but evinced no inclination to stray off in the darkness, *clustered on the far side of the fire*," the sentence would contain a dangling modifier, as readers may be unsure if "clustered on the far side of the fire" is meant to describe the darkness or the wolf-dogs. By placing this descriptive phrase next to the noun it is intended to describe, London avoids this potential dangling modifier and provides readers with a clear and descriptive sentence.

Another example from *White Fang* that contains clearly placed descriptive language is the sentence "A few minutes later, Henry, who was now traveling behind the sled, emitted a low, warning whistle" (p. 185). As in the previous example, London situates "who was now traveling behind the sled" next to "Henry" to indicate that this description is meant to refer to him. If London placed the clause "who was now traveling behind the sled" at the end of the sentence, producing, "A few minutes later, Henry emitted a low, warning whistle, *who was now traveling behind the sled*," readers would likely be confused. Some readers of this new sentence might think that only the whistle was traveling behind the sled, while others might determine that this clause still refers to Henry and wonder why it is located in this unusual, "dangling" position at the end of the sentence. Fortunately, London ensures that this sentence from *White Fang* will not result in any such confusion by placing the clause "who was now traveling behind the sled" next to the noun to which it refers.

These examples from *White Fang* illustrate the importance of avoiding dangling modifiers. The descriptive elements in Jack London's original sentences provide important details that can further enhance a reader's understanding of a situation described in the text. However, if the phrases and clauses London uses to provide additional detail are positioned as dangling modifiers, they detract from the quality of the sentences in which they appear instead of adding to them. By avoiding dangling modifiers, writers can ensure that the descriptive elements they include in their writing allow for their pieces to be both detailed and clear. Next, we will take a look inside a seventh-grade classroom and examine an activity I used to help my students understand the importance of avoiding dangling modifiers.

 ## A Classroom Snapshot

I begin today's class by letting my students know that we will be continuing our discussion of dangling modifiers. This class period marks the third time these seventh graders and I have discussed this concept. When we first addressed the topic, I introduced the students to the basics of what dangling modifiers are, how they can appear in writing, and how they can be corrected. When we discussed this topic a second time, I showed students examples of effectively used phrases and clauses in literature and then rearranged those sentences so that they could see how those texts would be different if they featured dangling modifiers instead of correctly used ones. I tell the students that in today's class they will work in groups and analyze the differences between the original sentences from literature we examined in our last class and reworked versions of those sentences that included dangling modifiers.

I begin this activity by placing the chart depicted in Figure 6.4 on the document camera. In this chart, each sentence is displayed as it originally appears as well as how it would appear if it was reorganized to contain a dangling modifier. Two of the sentences in this chart are the examples from *White Fang* featured in the previous section, while two are from Donna Jo Napoli's (1998) novel *Sirena*.

I read these examples to the students, highlighting the dangling modifiers, and then give them directions about how the activity will work. I tell the

Original Sentences	Sentences with Dangling Modifiers
1. "The wolf-dogs, clustered on the far side of the fire, snarled and bickered among themselves, but evinced no inclination to stray off in the darkness," *White Fang* by Jack London, p. 172.	1. The wolf-dogs snarled and bickered among themselves, but evinced no inclination to stray off in the darkness, *clustered on the far side of the fire.*
2. "A few minutes later, Henry, who was now traveling behind the sled, emitted a low, warning whistle," *White Fang* by Jack London, p. 185.	2. A few minutes later, Henry emitted a low, warning whistle, *who was now traveling behind the sled.*
3. "Our island, which was once a mass of fragrant yellow lilies, has become an open graveyard," *Sirena* by Donna Jo Napoli, p. 19.	3. Our island has become an open graveyard, *which was once a mass of fragrant yellow lilies.*
4. "Philoctetes gets up and goes to his wooden chest, dug halfway into the ground among the bushes," *Sirena* by Donna Jo Napoli, p. 116.	4. *Dug halfway into the ground among the bushes,* Philoctetes gets up and goes to his wooden chest.

Figure 6.4 Sentences without and with Dangling Modifiers.

students that they will work in four groups and each group will be responsible for explaining the differences between an original sentence and the version of that sentence that contains a dangling modifier. "Your task," I explain, "is to tell all of us how the dangling modifier changes the sentence. Compare the original sentence with the one with a dangling modifier. What does the dangling modifier do to the meaning of that sentence? Once everyone is done, we'll hear from each group. You'll read us your original sentence, then the one with the dangling modifier, and, most importantly, you'll explain how the dangling modifier changes the sentence." I divide the students into four groups and give each group a piece of paper, on which is written an original sentence from Figure 6.4 and that sentence adapted to include a dangling modifier

Once the students have their sentences and are working in their groups, I check in with them to see how they are progressing. I begin by sitting down with the fourth group, which is working on the original sentence "Philoctetes gets up and goes to his wooden chest, dug halfway into the ground among the bushes" from *Sirena* and its revised version, "*Dug halfway into the ground among the bushes,* Philoctetes gets up and goes to his wooden chest." I immediately note that these students are doing a great job discussing the differences between the sentences. One student states, "The second version's confusing because of the dangling modifier. You don't know if (the modifier) is talking about the chest or about Philoctetes." Another student concurs and elaborates: "Yeah. The big difference is figuring out what's 'dug halfway into the ground among the bushes.' It's really the chest, but the second sentence makes it seem like it's Philoctetes." Impressed by these students' comments, I commend their excellent work and continue to move around the room.

Once I have checked in with the student groups and heard their ideas, I announce that it is time for each group to share its analysis with the class. Groups one through four go in order, with each group reading its sentences out loud (both the original version and the one with the dangling modifier) and analyzing how the dangling modifier impacts the meaning of the sentence. Group one compares the original sentence "The wolf-dogs, clustered on the far side of the fire, snarled and bickered among themselves, but evinced no inclination to stray off in the darkness" from *White Fang*, with the altered version, "The wolf-dogs snarled and bickered among themselves, but evinced no inclination to stray off in the darkness, *clustered on the far side of the fire*." One of the members of this group notes, "The dangling modifier is really important here because of how confusing it makes the second sentence. 'Clustered on the far side of the fire' is a dangling modifier in the second sentence. This sentence, because of how it's written with the dangling modifier, sounds like the darkness is what's clustered on the far side of the fire, but it's not. The wolf-dogs are clustered there. The first sentence, the one without the dangling modifier, shows this much better."

"Very good analysis," I respond. "You did a great job of saying how the dangling modifier impacts the meaning of the second sentence. Really nice work."

Recommendations for Teaching Students about Recognizing and Correcting Dangling Modifiers

In this section, I describe a step-by-step instructional process to use when teaching students to recognize and correct dangling modifiers. The instructional steps I recommend are: (1) show students examples from literature of effectively used phrases and clauses; (2) show students how those examples would look with dangling modifiers; (3) have students analyze the differences between the original sentences and those with dangling modifiers; (4) ask students to use descriptive elements in their own writing while making sure to avoid dangling modifiers; and (5) ask students to reflect on why correcting dangling modifiers is important. Since this instructional process is designed to help students apply their knowledge of dangling modifiers and think analytically about the importance of this concept, I recommend using the information at the beginning of this chapter, such as the definitions, examples, and correction strategies, to ensure that students understand the fundamentals of dangling modifiers before beginning these activities.

1. Show Students Examples from Literature of Effectively Used Phrases and Clauses

The first step in this instructional process is showing students modifiers that *are not* dangling by providing them with examples from literature of effectively used phrases and clauses. Doing so not only shows students the correct usage of these modifiers, but also provides them with the understandings that they will need later in this instructional process when they compare correctly used modifiers with dangling ones. When showing students these examples, I recommend prominently displaying (on the document camera, overhead projector, or whiteboard) a sentence from literature that contains a descriptive phrase or clause. Once all the students can see the sentence, point out the descriptive element in it and engage the students in a discussion about what that element is describing. For example, I have shown my students the following sentence (also depicted in Figure 6.4) from Donna Jo Napoli's novel *Sirena*: "Our island, which was once a mass of fragrant yellow lilies, has become an open graveyard" (p. 19). After displaying the sentence, I pointed out the descriptive clause "which was once a mass of fragrant yellow lilies" and talked with the students about what the clause is meant to describe. Once the students were able to explain to me that this clause provides more detail about the "island," I knew we were ready to move to the next step of the process.

2. Show Students How Those Examples Would Look with Dangling Modifiers

The next step of this instructional process is to show students how these examples from literature would look if they were reworked to include dangling modifiers. For example, the sentence "Our island, which was once a mass of fragrant yellow lilies, has become an open graveyard" from *Sirena* could be reconfigured as follows to include a dangling modifier: "Our island has become an open graveyard, which was once a mass of fragrant yellow lilies." To create this new version, I moved the clause "which was once a mass of fragrant yellow lilies" from its original position following "island" to the end of the sentence. While the original sentence clearly indicates that this clause is meant to describe "island," the new version is not so clear; readers could be confused by the clause's placement and not know if it is supposed to describe "island," "graveyard," or both. When I recently showed this sentence to my students, I called their attention to its new configuration and explained to them that this is an example of a dangling modifier. "We say this clause 'dangles,'" I explained, "because it's hard to tell what it's actually describing." I continued to show them the rest of the sentences in Figure 6.4, pointing out the dangling modifier in each situation. Once I showed the students these sentences, I told them that we would return to them in the next activity, which is also the third step of this instructional process.

3. Have Students Analyze the Differences between the Original Sentences and Those with Dangling Modifiers

The third step in this instructional process is to ask students to analyze the differences between the original sentences and those with dangling modifiers. This step extends from the first two in this process: since the first step involves showing the students correctly written examples and the second calls for showing them revised versions of those examples with dangling modifiers, the third step is the time to ask students to analyze the differences between those sentences. As illustrated in the classroom snapshot, I recommend dividing the students into groups and making each group responsible for analyzing the differences between an original sentence from literature and a new version of that sentence that contains a dangling modifier. When I engage my students in this activity, I tell them that their main task is to explain how the dangling modifier changes the sentence. There is no one right or wrong answer in this activity—it is based entirely on the students' analyses of each sentence. I like to give each group a piece of paper with the original and reworked versions of their sentences and then allow them to work collaboratively on their analyses. As the students discuss the differences in these sentences, I like to sit down and listen to their ideas, supporting them as needed. Once the students have come up with their analyses, I recommend asking each group to share its ideas verbally by having one or more group members first read the group's original sentence out loud, then do the same with the dangling modifier sentence, and then finally explain the differences between them, highlighting how the dangling modifier impacts the meaning of the second sentence. By sharing this analysis, students can illustrate the importance of recognizing and correcting dangling modifiers.

4. Ask Students to Use Descriptive Elements in Their Own Writing while Making Sure to Avoid Dangling Modifiers

The fourth step in this instructional process asks students to apply what they have learned about dangling modifiers to their own writing. To do this, have the students use descriptive elements in their own writing while making sure to avoid dangling modifiers. When I ask my students to work on applying this concept to their own works, I review with them examples of sentences that contain dangling modifiers, such as those in which the modifier is not placed next to the nouns it is describing and those in which the noun being described is not included in the sentence at all. Once I have reviewed this information in a whole-class mini lesson, I conference with the students individually as they write. I focus these conferences on the descriptive elements that the students are using in their writing and whether or not these modifiers clearly describe what they are intended. To facilitate these conversations, I ask each student to do three things: (1) find a sentence modifier in their work; (2) explain what it modifies; and (3) explain why it is clearly used (and therefore not dangling). If students can do these things, then I can leave the conference confident in their abilities to use descriptive elements in their writing and avoid dangling modifiers.

5. Ask Students to Reflect on Why Correcting Dangling Modifiers Is Important

Once students have completed these activities, I recommend concluding this instructional process by asking them for a final reflection on why it is important to correct dangling modifiers. Reflection such as this can help students think critically about why grammatical concepts such as this one are important to effective writing. If students think critically about elements of grammar, they can clearly see grammatical concepts as tools for effective writing. One way to facilitate this kind of reflection in your students is to post the following questions on the board and ask them to respond:

- ◆ What would it be like to read a piece of writing with a lot of dangling modifiers?
- ◆ Why is it important that writers make sure their works do not have dangling modifiers in them?

As your students answer these questions, you will want to help them get to the point where they understand that writers avoid dangling modifiers to maximize the clarity of their works. During a recent conversation about these questions, one student explained, "It's good to use modifiers, but they gotta make sense. If you read something where the author used dangling modifiers, the writing is worse, not better, because it's hard to understand something if it has dangling modifiers in it." As this student expressed, a piece of writing with a number of dangling modifiers would be difficult to understand and therefore not very enjoyable to read. Since writers want to convey their ideas clearly to readers, it is important that they recognize and correct dangling modifiers.

Final Thoughts on Recognizing and Correcting Dangling Modifiers

- Recognizing and correcting dangling modifiers is an element of grammar addressed in Common Core Language Standard 7.1.
- A modifier is an element of a sentence (such as a word, phrase, or clause) that adds detail.
  - Two especially important modifiers that authors use to add significant details are relative clauses and participial phrases.
- Dangling modifiers are descriptive aspects of sentences that are unclear in what they describe.
- There are two main ways dangling modifiers manifest themselves in writing:
  - The modifier is not placed next to the noun it is describing.
  - The noun being described is not included in the sentence at all.
- It is important that writers are able to recognize and correct dangling modifiers in their works in order to maximize the clarity of their writing.
- When teaching students about recognizing and correcting dangling modifiers:
  - Show students examples of effectively used phrases and clauses in literature.
  - Show students how those examples would look with dangling modifiers.
  - Have students analyze the differences between the original sentences and those with dangling modifiers.
  - Ask students to use descriptive elements in their own writing while making sure to avoid dangling modifiers.
  - Ask students to reflect on why correcting dangling modifiers is important.

Figure 6.5 depicts this instructional process in an easy-to-follow flowchart.

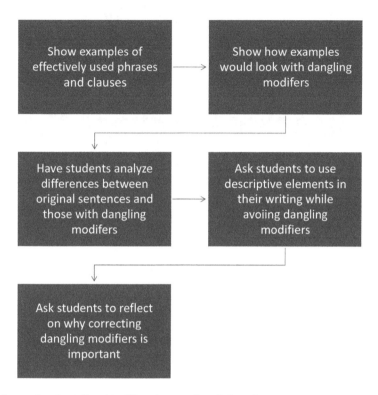

Figure 6.5 Correcting Dangling Modifiers Instructional Flowchart.

7

Choosing Language that Expresses Ideas Precisely and Eliminates Wordiness and Redundancy

What Does It Mean to Choose Language that Expresses Ideas Precisely and Eliminates Wordiness and Redundancy?

Common Core Language Standard 7.3 calls for students to "Choose language that expresses ideas precisely and concisely, recognizing and eliminating wordiness and redundancy" (Common Core State Standards Initiative, 2010). Regardless of a specific state's Common Core alignment, this topic is an important issue in writing instruction: while we frequently want our students to write descriptively, we do not want them to use a number of words that mean the same thing or use several words when one more specific one could achieve the same result. Instead, we want them to use language that conveys what they are trying to say as clearly as possible. For example, we might suggest our students use the word "jet" instead of "really fast plane" or that they write that characters "whispered" something rather than saying they "said it very quietly." Two especially important grammatical concepts related to this standard are specific nouns and strong verbs, as each of these can help writers express their ideas clearly while eliminating wordiness and redundancy. Let us explore each of these concepts in more depth.

Specific Nouns

Specific nouns eliminate wordiness because they clearly describe the object to which the author is referring. The previously used example of writing "jet" instead of "very fast plane" is a situation in which a specific noun can make a piece of writing as concise as possible. Sometimes, students will use a general noun combined with one or more adjectives rather than using one specific noun. It is our job as teachers to help students understand the benefits that come from using specific nouns instead: specific nouns make writing as concise and clear as possible and eliminate the wordiness that comes with using a general noun and a series of adjectives. Figure 7.1 contains some wordy descriptions of objects, along with specific nouns that can concisely replace them.

Strong Verbs

Strong verbs are similar to specific nouns; just as specific nouns describe objects clearly and precisely, strong verbs do the same thing with actions. Students will sometimes use a vague (or "weak") verb with one or more adverbs, when a strong verb will communicate the information in a more concise way. The previously used example of writing that characters "whispered" something instead of saying they "said it very quietly" is one way that a strong verb can express an action clearly while eliminating redundancy. When students learn more strong verbs, their writing will become more concise and direct, as they will be able to express specific actions without relying on wordy modifiers such as "really" and "very" to describe them. For example, saying that characters "dashed" out of a room is more exact and concise then saying they "went really quickly" out of it. Figure 7.2 contains some wordy descriptions of actions, along with strong verbs that can replace them.

Wordy Descriptions of Objects	Specific Noun Replacements
Really tall building	Skyscraper
The people to whom I am related	Family
Place used for growing plants	Garden

Figure 7.1 Wordy Descriptions and Specific Noun Replacements.

Wordy Descriptions of Actions	Strong Verb Replacements
Threw very gently	Tossed
Walked slowly	Strolled
Ate very quickly	Devoured

Figure 7.2 Wordy Descriptions and Strong Verb Replacements.

In the next section, we will examine why choosing language that expresses ideas precisely and eliminates wordiness is important to good writing. As part of this, we will look at how a published author uses specific nouns and strong verbs in one of her books and unpack the importance of those language choices.

Why Choosing Language that Expresses Ideas Precisely and Eliminates Wordiness Is Important to Good Writing

Choosing language that expresses ideas precisely and eliminates wordiness is a key element of effective writing. Writers who use specific nouns and strong verbs ensure that they are clearly describing the objects and actions about which they are writing. Vague nouns and weak verbs can lead to readers being confused and possibly not envisioning what the writer actually intended. For example, a writer may refer to "a very small dog" in a piece. Since there are many kinds of small dogs, readers may envision a kind of small dog that was different from what the writer intended. However, if the writer referred to a specific kind of small dog, such as a Chihuahua, then the reader and writer would be certain to envision the same thing. In addition, writers who use vague nouns and weak verbs often use more words in their writing than necessary. William Strunk and E.B. White, in their 1959 book *The Elements of Style*, advocated for writers expressing themselves clearly and without excess language:

> A sentence should contain no unnecessary words, a paragraph no unnecessary sentences, for the same reason that a drawing should have no unnecessary lines and a machine no unnecessary parts. This requires not that the writer make all his sentences short … but that every word tell.
>
> (p. 21)

When writers choose language that expresses ideas precisely, such as by using strong verbs and specific nouns, they ensure that every word they use "tells," or clearly communicates important information.

Let us take a look at how Suzanne Collins uses strong verbs and specific nouns in her 2008 book *The Hunger Games* and why these language choices are important to the effectiveness of the novel. Collins uses the strong verb "hurries" in the following sentence, in which Katniss Everdeen, the book's narrator and protagonist, is describing her interactions with Effie Trinket, a woman responsible for escorting Katniss and her counterpart Peeta to the Hunger Games: "Then (Effie) kisses us each on the cheek and hurries out" (p. 138). The verb "hurries" is important to this sentence, as it depicts the action clearly and concisely. If Collins had chosen to have Katniss narrate this action using a different verb, we readers might not have the clear understanding of the scene that we currently do. For example, if we were told that Effie "kisses us each on the cheek and then goes out," we would not have a clear understanding of how she left. If we were instead informed that Effie "kisses us each on the cheek and then goes quickly out," we would have a clear understanding of Effie's actions, but the text would be wordier then it originally was. The use of the strong verb "hurries" allows readers to clearly envision the way the action took place while also eliminating unnecessary wordiness.

Collins also uses specific nouns to maximize clarity and guard against wordiness in *The Hunger Games*. When Katniss discusses her interactions with her sister's cat, Buttercup, she explains, "Sometimes, when I clean a kill, I feed Buttercup the entrails" (p. 4). In this sentence, Collins has Katniss use the specific noun "entrails" to depict the situation clearly and concisely. If Katniss had instead said "the insides of the animal" or "the animal's internal organs," the information conveyed in this sentence would be wordier and less direct as it currently is. At another point in the book, Collins has Katniss use the specific noun "hovercraft" to allow readers to clearly envision a particular object. The sentence "The hovercraft appears a hundred yards or so away" (p. 318) is made clear by the specificity of "hovercraft"; if the sentence used vaguer and wordier language, such as "flying object" or "mode of transportation," it would be much more difficult for readers to envision the situation as the author intended. The use of this specific noun makes this sentence as clear and concise as possible.

These examples from *The Hunger Games* illustrate the importance of choosing language that expresses ideas precisely and eliminates unnecessary wordiness. The strong verbs and specific nouns Suzanne Collins uses in this book contribute to its effectiveness; without them, the book would not make its points as clearly and concisely. With these strong verbs and specific nouns, readers can clearly envision the action and images as Collins intended. Now, let us take a look inside a seventh-grade classroom and see how these students and I explored this standard and the language choices that are essential to it.

A Classroom Snapshot

As my seventh graders enter the classroom, take their seats, and look up at the projector screen at the front of the room to see prominently displayed sentences from *The Hunger Games*, I greet the students and then explain the activity: "Today, we're going to look at these sentences from *The Hunger Games* while thinking about the subject we started exploring last class: using specific nouns and strong verbs. I've displayed these sentences on the projector screen because they're good examples of sentences with specific nouns or strong verbs." I point to the projector screen at the front of the classroom, which contains the heading "Two Sentences from *The Hunger Games*" and the sentences "In the fall, a few brave souls sneak into the woods to harvest apples" (p. 6) and "I finally had to kill the lynx because he scared off game" (p. 7).

"Let's start with the first one," I state, motioning towards the sentence "In the fall, a few brave souls sneak into the woods to harvest apples." "Suzanne Collins, the author of *The Hunger Games*, is a great writer," I begin. "What's really cool about looking at her work like this is that we can see some of the reasons why she's so good. She can definitely tell a great story, but she is also ireally good at using strong verbs and specific nouns. In this sentence, let's focus on the strong verb 'sneak' that Collins uses. 'Sneak' is a really good example of a strong verb because it lets us, as readers, picture exactly how the action happened. When we read that these 'brave souls sneak into the woods,' we know exactly how they go into the woods. They're not walking slowly, and they're not making a lot of noise. They're quickly and quietly going into the woods."

I take a step towards an easel pad at the front of the classroom and tell the students, "Now, let's take a look at what this sentence might look like if it didn't use the strong verb 'sneak.'" I write on the easel pad, "In the fall, a few brave souls *go* into the woods to harvest apples," underlining the word "go" as I write it. I read the sentence out loud and ask the class, "What's different about this sentence?"

"It says 'go' instead of 'sneak,'" replies one student.

"You're absolutely right," I respond. "How does this change the sentence?"

"'Go' isn't specific," answers the student. "There are a bunch of ways you can 'go.'"

I affirm the student's statement: "That's a very good point. You could 'go' in a number of ways. You can go somewhere slowly, quickly, quietly, noisily. The word 'sneak' paints a much clearer image in our mind. Now, I'm going to change this sentence again and ask you what you think." I turn to a new page on the easel pad and write, "In the fall, a few brave souls *go quickly and quietly* into the woods to harvest apples." I read it aloud and ask the students, "What do you think of this version?"

A number of students raise their hands; I call on a young lady who states, "This one's clearer than the last one you wrote because it describes the way the people 'go.' It says they go 'quickly and quietly.'"

"Very good," I reply. "Let's compare this one with the original sentence that uses the strong verb 'sneak.' Why might Suzanne Collins have used 'sneak' instead of 'go quickly and quietly?'"

A student explains: "'Sneak' doesn't use as many words to say the same thing. She probably said sneak so that she didn't have to use as many words to say it."

"Excellent," I respond. "One reason to use a strong verb like 'sneak' is to eliminate wordiness in one's writing. You did a great job of describing that." Next, I tell the students that we will be transitioning to thinking about specific nouns using the sentence "I finally had to kill the lynx because he scared off game" from *The Hunger Games*. "Can anyone point out a specific noun in this sentence?"

A student answers: "'Lynx' is a specific noun. It's a kind of wildcat."

"That's right," I say. "A lynx is a medium-sized wildcat. Let's look at how this sentence would read if Collins used 'medium-sized wildcat' instead of 'lynx.'" I rewrite the sentence on the easel pad, making this substitution, and creating the sentence "I finally had to kill the *medium-sized wildcat* because he scared off game." After I read the sentence out loud, I ask the students for their thoughts.

"I don't like this sentence as much as the first one," offers one student. "Using the word 'lynx' just makes it sound so much better."

I follow up: "Why do you think that word improves the sentence?"

"It's not so vague. 'Medium-sized wildcat' is really vague. 'Lynx' isn't."

"Good," I reply. "'Lynx' is much more specific. How about the issue of wordiness here? Is one of these wordier than the other?"

"'Medium-sized wildcat' is much wordier," another student volunteers. "It uses a lot more words to tell you what had to be killed."

"Excellent!" I respond. "You all did great work thinking about these sentences. When you write, make sure you use strong verbs and specific nouns. They make your point as clearly as possible and eliminate extra words. Very nice work today!"

Recommendations for Teaching Students to Choose Language that Expresses Ideas Precisely and Eliminates Wordiness and Redundancy

In this section, I describe a step-by-step instructional process to use when teaching students to improve their writing by using specific nouns and strong verbs. Using these concepts allows students to meet Common Core Language Standard 7.3's requirement that students "Choose language that expresses ideas precisely and concisely, recognizing and eliminating wordiness and redundancy." The instructional steps I recommend are: (1) show students examples of specific nouns and strong verbs from published works; (2) change these examples to contain vaguer nouns and weaker verbs and discuss the differences; (3) ask students to create sentences with and without specific nouns and strong verbs and analyze the differences; (4) have students focus on using specific nouns and strong verbs while working on their own writing; and (5) ask students to reflect on why specific nouns and strong verbs are important to effective writing. Since this instructional process is designed to help students apply their knowledge of specific nouns and strong verbs and think analytically about how they express ideas precisely while eliminating unnecessary wordiness, I recommend using the information at the beginning of this chapter, such as the explanations of specific nouns and strong verbs and the examples found in Figures 7.1 and 7.2, to ensure students understand these concepts before beginning these instructional activities.

1. Show Students Examples of Specific Nouns and Strong Verbs from Published Works

The first step in this instructional process is to show students mentor texts of specific nouns and strong verbs—published works in which authors effectively use these concepts. I recommend showing students that strong verbs and specific nouns are present in a wide range of texts; I have found that when students see that writers across genres use strong verbs and specific nouns, they understand that these are important concepts for all types of writing. Once students understand this, I encourage them to use strong verbs and specific nouns in everything they write: short stories, research reports, argumentative essays, poems, and any other genres in which they work. For example, when recently talking with students about how writers in all genres use strong verbs and specific nouns, I showed them examples of these concepts from an autobiography written by Supreme Court Justice Sonia Sotomayor titled *The Beloved World of Sonia Sotomayor* (2018). This book, like many well-written texts, uses strong verbs and specific nouns effectively to express ideas clearly and eliminate wordiness. When talking about strong verbs, I showed students the excerpt "I was a watchful child constantly scanning the adults for clues and listening in on their conversations" (p. 18), focusing on the strong verb "scanning." I highlighted the way this verb conveys to the reader the exact way Sotomayor looked at the adults she describes and the clear mental image it provides. When talking about specific nouns, I discussed the following passage, in which Sotomayor recounts her memories of her father providing her with medical attention: "When my father made his first attempt at giving me the insulin shot the day before, his hands were shaking so much I was afraid he would miss my arm and stab me in the face"

(p. 5). When sharing this selection, I focused on the specific noun "insulin," discussing how Sotomayor uses it to clearly indicate the kind of medication her father tried to give her.

2. Change These Examples to Contain Vaguer Nouns and Weaker Verbs and Discuss the Differences

In this step, I recommend changing the published examples you have shown your students so that these sentences contain vaguer nouns and weaker verbs. For example, after showing students the passage "I was a watchful child constantly scanning the adults for clues and listening in on their conversations" (p. 18), I rewrote it as "I was a watchful child constantly *looking closely at* the adults for clues and listening in on their conversations" and talked with the students about how this version of the sentence differs from the original. I pointed out how "looking closely" is wordier than "scanning" and does not create as clear a mental image. Similarly, I illustrated the importance of specific nouns by showing students the sentence "When my father made his first attempt at giving me the insulin shot the day before, his hands were shaking so much I was afraid he would miss my arm and stab me in the face" (p. 5) and then rewriting it as "When my father made his first attempt at giving me the *diabetes medication* shot the day before, his hands were shaking so much I was afraid he would miss my arm and stab me in the face." I talked with the students about how the specific noun "insulin" is a more precise and less wordy way of providing the readers with the intended information. I then followed up by explaining to them that writing that uses strong verbs and specific nouns such as those Sotomayor includes in her book can clearly express information without using a lot of extra words.

3. Ask Students to Create Sentences with and without Specific Nouns and Strong Verbs and Analyze the Differences

For the next step in this process, I recommend asking students to take even more ownership of their learning by creating their own sentences that contain specific nouns and strong verbs, revising them so that they no longer contain those concepts, and considering the differences. When I do this, I give the students a chart that asks them to: (1) write a sentence with a specific noun; (2) rewrite the sentence with the specific noun replaced by a vague noun and adjective; and (3) explain how the sentences seem different. I also give the students a chart that asks them to do a similar activity with strong verbs; this chart calls for the students to: (1) write a sentence with a strong verb; (2) rewrite the sentence with the strong verb replaced by a weak one and an adverb; and (3) explain how the sentences seem different. Figures 7.3 and 7.4 show these charts completed by a student named Erica. Blank and

Sentence with a Strong Verb	Rewritten Sentence with the Strong Verb Replaced by a Weak Verb and an Adverb	How You Think the Sentences are Different
The batter <u>sprinted</u> to first base.	The batter <u>ran quickly</u> to first base.	The sentence with the strong verb is more specific and less wordy.

Figure 7.3 Example of Strong Verb Chart.

Sentence with a Specific Noun	Rewritten Sentence with the Specific Noun Replaced by a Vague Noun and an Adjective	How You Think The Sentences are Different
We did <u>experiments</u> on our field trip.	We did <u>many things</u> on our school field trip.	The sentence with the specific noun is less wordy and more clear.

Figure 7.4 Example of Specific Noun Chart.

reproducible versions of these charts that you can use in your classroom are available in the appendix.

4. Have Students Focus on Using Specific Nouns and Strong Verbs while Working on Their Own Writing

Now that students have practiced creating sentences with specific nouns and strong verbs, the next step is to ask them to apply those skills to their own writing. I have found this to be a beneficial instructional practice because it requires the students to use these grammatical concepts in an authentic setting: a piece of writing on which they are currently working. Before the students write, I recommend conducting a brief mini-lesson for the class in which you remind them of the ways strong verbs and specific nouns enhance a piece of writing and review with them some examples of these concepts. After this, the students are ready to work independently on their own written works. I suggest holding one-on-one conferences with students while they write. During these conferences, I like to ask students to show me an example of a strong verb and a specific noun in their works so that I can see that they understand these grammatical tools and are using them effectively. If a student shows me a strong verb that is actually a weak one, or a specific noun that is actually vague, I do some remediation with the student by reviewing the concept in more depth and discussing additional examples until the student understands. These one-on-one conferences are excellent opportunities to see how well each student understands these concepts and to rectify any misunderstandings.

5. Ask Students to Reflect on Why Specific Nouns and Strong Verbs Are Important to Effective Writing

The final step of this instructional process is to ask students to reflect on why specific nouns and strong verbs are important to effective writing. I have found that engaging students in this kind of reflection helps them understand the "grammar as a set of tools" metaphor; when students consider the importance of a particular grammatical concept to good writing, they develop a deeper understanding of why published authors use it in their works and how they can use it themselves to enhance their own writing. To facilitate this kind of analysis, I recommend asking students to reflect on the question: "Why are specific nouns and strong verbs important to good writing?" A seventh grader with whom I recently worked pointed out that specific nouns and strong verbs are important concepts because they "make writing as clear as possible." This student continued to note that, "If you didn't use (specific nouns and strong verbs), your writing wouldn't be good. It would be unclear and might be too wordy."

Final Thoughts on Using Language that Expresses Ideas Precisely and Eliminates Wordiness and Redundancy

- Common Core Language Standard 7.3 calls for students to "Choose language that expresses ideas precisely and concisely, recognizing and eliminating wordiness and redundancy."
- Two especially important grammatical concepts related to this standard are specific nouns and strong verbs, as each of these can help writers express their ideas clearly while eliminating wordiness and redundancy:
    - Specific nouns clearly describe the object to which the author is referring (as compared to vague nouns, which do not describe objects as clearly and often need adjectives to accompany them).
    - Strong verbs describe actions clearly and precisely. While students sometimes use a vague (or "weak") verb with one or more adverbs, a strong verb will communicate the information in a more concise way.
- Choosing language that expresses ideas precisely and eliminates wordiness is a key element of effective writing. Writers who use specific nouns and strong verbs ensure that they are clearly describing the objects and actions about which they are writing.
- When teaching students about specific nouns and strong verbs:
    - Show students examples of specific nouns and strong verbs from published works.
    - Change these examples to contain vaguer nouns and weaker verbs and discuss the differences.
    - Ask students to create sentences with and without specific nouns and strong verbs and analyze the differences.
    - Have students focus on using specific nouns and strong verbs while working on their own writing.
    - Ask students to reflect on why specific nouns and strong verbs are important to effective writing.

Figure 7.5 depicts this instructional process in an easy-to-follow flowchart.

Choosing Language that Expresses Ideas ◆ 101

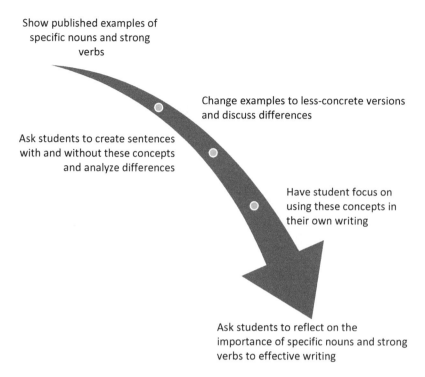

Figure 7.5 Precise Language Instructional Flowchart.

8

Distinguishing among Connotations of Words with Similar Denotations

What Are Connotations and Denotations?

Common Core Language Standard 7.5 calls for students to "Distinguish among the connotations (associations) of words with similar denotations (definitions) (e.g., *refined, respectful, polite, diplomatic, condescending*)" (Common Core State Standards Initiative, 2010). Let us begin our discussion of this standard by using some examples to further unpack the differences between connotations and denotations. As this standard explains, connotations are the associations we make with particular words while denotations are the dictionary definitions of those words. Many words with similar denotations might have very different connotations. For example, the words "pushy" and "assertive" are both used to describe people who aggressively advocate for what they want. However, "pushy" has a negative connotation, while "assertive" has a positive one. The word "pushy" is typically associated with obnoxiously aggressive behavior, while "assertive" is often associated with confidence. Figure 8.1 presents, in chart form, the similar denotation and distinct connotations of these two words.

Two other words with similar denotations but different connotations are "cheap" and "frugal." While both of these words are used to describe someone who is cautious about spending money, "cheap" carries a negative connotation while "frugal" carries a more positive one. The word "cheap" is associated with being stingy or selfish, while "frugal" is associated with

Word	Denotation	Connotation
Pushy	Adjective used to describe someone who aggressively advocates for what he or she wants.	This word has a negative connotation. It is associated with obnoxiously aggressive behavior.
Assertive	Adjective used to describe someone who aggressively advocates for what he or she wants.	This word has a positive connotation. It is associated with confidence.

Figure 8.1 Denotations and Connotations of "Pushy" and "Assertive."

Word	Denotation	Connotation
Cheap	Adjective used to describe someone who is cautious about spending money.	This word has a negative connotation. It is associated with being stingy or selfish.
Frugal	Adjective used to describe someone who is cautious about spending money.	This word has a positive connotation. It is associated with being careful and not wasting money.

Figure 8.2 Denotations and Connotations of "Cheap" and "Frugal."

being careful and not wasting money. Figure 8.2 presents the denotation and connotation of these two words.

Why Distinguishing among Connotations of Words with Similar Denotations Is Important to Good Writing

An effective writer needs to understand that words with similar denotations can have very different connotations. Good writers are aware of the kind of tone they are creating in their writing and are sure that the words they select have connotations that align with that tone. For example, a writer who is creating a positive tone about a character might use "quiet" instead of "timid," as "timid" is associated with being fearful while "quiet" is not. I have seen the importance of this grammatical concept emerge when working with middle school students on their writing. When conferencing with a student, I noticed that she used the word "thin" frequently and suggested that she replace some of those words with synonyms. The student consulted a thesaurus and told me that she was going to replace some of the uses of "thin" with "scrawny." We then had a conversation about the difference between denotation and connotation and discussed the connotation associated with the word "scrawny." Once this student understood that "scrawny" did not align with the tone of her piece, she explained that she was going to use "lean," a word that carries the connotation she was looking for.

In this section, we will take a look at how some published writers purposefully select words that carry specific connotations and consider how their works would be different if they chose words that had different connotations instead. In the 2004 novel *Midnighters: The Secret Hour*, Scott Westerfield describes a family's experience moving to a new town, which turns out to have strong supernatural elements. Much of this book has an ominous and foreboding tone, and Westerfield skillfully chooses words with connotations that match that tone. When describing the experience of Jessica Day, the book's main character, waking up in the middle of the night, Westerfield writes, "It wasn't just the unfamiliar house; the Oklahoma night itself felt wrong" (p. 16). In this sentence, Westerfield uses the word "unfamiliar" to help achieve the uneasy tone that characterizes this passage. The word "unfamiliar" has more of a negative connotation than some other words and phrases that have similar denotations. For example, if Westerfield had written "new" instead, this sentence would not have the same effect because of the positive connotation of this term. In addition, the positive feelings associated with the phrase "new" would not align with the rest of the tone Westerfield is trying to create. While Jessica and her family are indeed living in a new house, Westerfield's selection of the word "unfamiliar" is most appropriate for this situation; it can inspire uneasiness and anxiety, two feelings that are associated with the scene described here.

Nonfiction authors pay attention to connotations and denotations as well. In the 1994 book *Predator*, an informational text about the experiences of predators in nature, author Bruce Brooks selects words with connotations that align with the tone he deems relevant to the animals he describes. For example, when placing the reader in the position of a leopard killing his prey, Brooks writes, "Not that you ever doubted your superior strength, or your speed, or your craftiness" (p. 29). If Brooks used "deceitfulness" instead of "craftiness," this sentence would take on a more negative tone. While "craftiness" and "deceitfulness" have similar denotations (they are both related to acts of deception), their connotations are different. "Craftiness" is associated with skill and cunning, while "deceitfulness" is more closely associated with outright lying. Since Brooks is emphasizing the leopard's cunning and intelligence, "craftiness" is the appropriate choice here.

A related example in *Predator* is found in the following passage, located in a section of the book that describes predatory animals' hunting strategies: "It is easy to see that many predatory animals are smart" (p. 13). This sentence would read quite differently if Brooks replaced "smart" with one of the many words that have a similar denotation but a different connotation. For example, the words "brainy" or "wise" have similar denotations to "smart," but would seem out of place in a chapter on predators' hunting strategies. "Brainy" has more of an intellectual connotation than "smart" does, and "wise" suggests someone who is quiet and contemplative. Compared to these other words, Brooks's choice of the word "smart" is much more aligned with the message he is trying to convey: that predatory animals are strategic, cunning, and crafty when hunting their prey.

As the examples discussed in this section illustrate, it is very important that writers distinguish among connotations of words with similar denotations. If an author chooses a word with a connotation that does not fit with the tone of a piece, readers may be confused and misinterpret the author's message. If Westerfield and Brooks had used words with similar denotations but different connotations in the passages described in this section, their works would not have been as effective. The best authors not only pay attention to the denotations of the words they use, but also to the connotations of them. Choosing words with connotations that best fit their desired tones allows for their works to be as effective as possible. Now let us take a look at an activity I did with a class of seventh graders that helped them understand the importance of paying attention to connotation when selecting a word.

A Classroom Snapshot

Today, my seventh graders and I are in our third day of discussing connotation and denotation, in conjunction with our work on the Common Core Language Standards. On the first day, we discussed the fundamentals of these concepts, such as what connotation and denotation mean, and looked at examples of words with similar denotations but different connotations. Then, on our second day discussing this topic, I showed the students a sentence from a book they had read earlier in the year, Todd Strasser's (1981) novel *The Wave*, and talked about the connotations of two of the words in that sentence. I showed them the sentence "On weekends he'd visit Indian reservations or spend hours looking for old books in dusty libraries" (p. 33), which describes how the book's main character, a high school history teacher named Ben Ross, researched a subject he was studying and teaching. When discussing this sentence, I focused on the words "old" and "dusty," explaining that each of these words was used to demonstrate that Ben was researching books that had been around for a long time.

In today's class, I explain to the students that we are going to look at this sentence again, but this time we will add another layer to our work: "Last time we met, we talked about a sentence from *The Wave*, and the connotations of two words in that sentence: 'old' and 'dusty.' We discussed how the words 'old' and 'dusty' are related to the age of the materials Ben Ross used in his research. These words show how thorough his research was, since he studied old and dusty things, not just new ones or ones that were easy to find. The sentence is on the easel pad up here in the front of the room so everyone can see it. Today, we're going to take that sentence and do something else with it. I'm going to ask you to work together with a partner and try to revise this sentence by replacing 'old' and 'dusty' with words that have similar denotations but different connotations." I conclude these directions by reviewing the difference between connotations and denotations and showing students the examples of each illustrated in Figures 8.1 and 8.2.

The students begin work on this activity, talking with their partners about words that could replace "old" and "dusty" in this sentence. I move around the classroom, taking note of what ideas the students are generating. My interest is particularly piqued by one pair who is working on coming up with a replacement for "dusty."

"'Dusty' means covered with dust," one student explains, "but its connotation is 'old,' like something that's dusty is old. If we said 'filthy' (as a replacement word), that would have a similar denotation, but a different connotation. 'Filthy' doesn't have the connotation of being old, it just means dirty."

"That's fantastic!" I exclaim. "You did an outstanding job of differentiating between connotation and denotation, and I love the way you pointed out that 'filthy' has a similar denotation but a very different connotation than 'dusty' does."

I continue to circulate around the room, making note of what students are saying. Another pair comes up with an intriguing replacement for "old," saying that they would like to replace it with "mature." When I ask them about this, one of the group members explains, "'Mature' has a denotation like 'old,' but its connotation isn't the same. It's associated with people, not with books, so it has a different connotation."

"A very good point," I respond. "Some words have connotations that you'd associate with different things. You might describe an older person as mature, but not an older book. These words have similar denotations, but, like you said, they're associated with different things, so they have different connotations."

I call the class together and ask for volunteer pairs to share the new sentences they created. The first group to volunteer is the one that replaced "dusty" with "filthy." One of the group's members shares its full sentence, saying, "On weekends he'd visit Indian reservations or spend hours looking for ancient books in filthy libraries."

I praise this group's work and ask them to provide even more insight into their choices: "Great job. Can you all tell us a little about the words you substituted for 'old' and 'dusty?'"

"We changed 'old' to 'ancient,'" one of the students shares, "because they have similar denotations, but different connotations. 'Ancient' is associated with something really old, so we thought it had a different connotation than 'old.'"

"Very nice," I respond. "Now, how about the word you used to replace 'dusty?'"

"We changed 'dusty' to 'filthy,'" explains the other student in the group. "'Dusty' and 'filthy' have similar denotations because they both mean something is dirty, but their connotations are different."

"Good," I reply. "How are they different?"

"The connotation of 'dusty' is 'old,' but the connotation of 'filthy' is just really dirty."

"Excellent," I respond. A number of other pairs volunteer to share their work, all demonstrating good understandings of the differences between connotations and denotations. After these other groups share, I praise their work: "Fantastic job today. You're really doing great work with connotations and denotations."

Recommendations for Teaching Students to Distinguish among Connotations of Words with Similar Denotations

In this section, I describe a step-by-step instructional process to use when teaching students to distinguish among connotations of words with similar denotations. The instructional steps I recommend are: (1) show students examples from literature of words with specific connotations and explain those connotations; (2) ask students to change key words in these examples so that they have different connotations; (3) ask students to create their own sentences, using words with specific connotations, and then replace those words; (4) have students work on their own writing, focusing on the connotations and denotations of their words; and (5) ask students to reflect on the importance of connotation. Since this instructional process is designed to help students apply their understandings of connotations and denotations, I recommend using the information from the beginning of this chapter, such as the examples in Figures 8.1 and 8.2 and the related definitions, to make sure students understand the fundamental components of connotation and denotation before beginning these instructional activities.

1. Show Students Examples from Literature of Words with Specific Connotations and Explain Those Connotations

The first step of this instructional process is to show students examples from literature of words with specific connotations and explain what those connotations are. While you will want to consider your own students' interests and reading levels when selecting mentor texts to show them, this chapter contains a number of potential examples you could use to illustrate this concept. Figure 8.3 contains the four "mentor" sentences used in this chapter to explain the importance of connotation, the key word I focused on when describing each sentence, and the connotation of that word.

You can use all four of these sentences to show students specific examples of published authors using words with particular connotations. I recommend showing each sentence to your students and then thinking aloud about the specific connotations of each of these key words and how they

Mentor Examples	**Key Words**	**Connotation of Key Words**
"It wasn't just the unfamiliar house; the Oklahoma night itself felt wrong," *Midnighters: The Secret Hour* by Scott Westerfield, p. 16.	Unfamiliar	"Unfamiliar" is associated with feelings of strangeness and uneasiness.
"Not that you ever doubted your superior strength, or your speed, or your craftiness," *Predator* by Bruce Brooks, p. 29.	Craftiness	"Craftiness" is associated with skill, cunning, and intelligence.
"It is easy to see that many predatory animals are smart," *Predator* by Bruce Brooks, p. 13.	Smart	"Smart" is associated with the strategy and cunning predatory animals use when hunting their prey.
"On weekends he'd visit Indian reservations or spend hours looking for old books in dusty libraries," *The Wave* by Todd Strasser, p. 33.	Old, dusty	"Old" and "dusty" are associated with the age of the materials used by the book's main character. They illustrate the thoroughness of his research.

Figure 8.3 Mentor Examples, Key Words, and the Connotations of those Words.

impact the sentences in which they appear. For example, when showing your students the sentence "It wasn't just the unfamiliar house; the Oklahoma night itself felt wrong," from *Midnighters: The Secret Hour*, you can tell your students how important it was that the author chose the word "unfamiliar" because of the way its connotation aligns with the tone of the rest of the sentence.

2. Ask Students to Change Key Words in These Examples so that They Have Different Connotations

The next step in this instructional process is to ask students to change key words in the examples you showed them. Specifically, the students should change these words into others that have similar denotations but different connotations. The classroom snapshot section contains an example of this activity: the students used the sentence "On weekends he'd visit Indian reservations or spend hours looking for old books in dusty libraries" from *The Wave* and changed "old" and "dusty" to words with similar denotations but different connotations. I have found that this step of the instructional process is beneficial because it requires the students to take an active role in their learning about connotation and denotation; by changing specific words to others with different connotations, they must think carefully about the connotations of potential replacement words and make choices accordingly. As the students share their new sentences, I recommend asking them to comment on their choices by explaining how the new words they included have different connotations from the original ones. This challenges students to reveal their thought processes and the reasons behind the choices they made.

3. Ask Students to Create Their Own Sentences, Using Words with Specific connotations, and Then Replace Those Words

In this step of the instructional process, students create a sentence that uses a word with a specific connotation, then rewrite the sentence, replacing that word with another that has a different connotation, and finally explain the differences between the original word and the one that replaced it. Because the students will have just done a similar activity with a published sentence, they will understand how to replace a word in an existing sentence with another that contains a similar denotation but a different connotation. However, since this activity calls for students to create their own sentences that they will then change, I like to give them some additional support by showing them a model. Figure 8.4 contains a model I have shown my students while preparing them for this activity. As you can see, it includes an original sentence with a key word underlined, a revised version of that sentence with the key word

Original Sentence	Sentence with a Word Replaced by Another with a Different Connotation	How the Connotation of Those Words Differ
We walked at a *leisurely* pace through the park.	We walked at a *slow* pace through the park.	"Leisurely" has a more positive connotation than "slow." In their sentences, "leisurely" is associated with relaxation, while "slow" is associated with boredom.

Figure 8.4 Model for Connotation Replacement.

replaced by another with a different connotation, and an explanation of how the connotations of those key words differ.

After I show my students these sentences and explain how the connotations of the highlighted words differ, I will ask them to work in small groups and complete this same activity. I will give each group a blank version of the chart depicted in Figure 8.4 (which can be found in the appendix) and ask them to fill it out. Once all of the groups are done, I will ask them to share their sentences and explanations with the class. I stress to my students that a very important part of this activity is explaining the differences in the connotations between the key words because their explanations reveal their understandings of the connotations of the words they selected.

4. Have Students Work on Their Own Writing, Focusing on the Connotations and Denotations of Their Words

The next step in this instructional process is to have students work on their own writing, focusing on the connotations and denotations of their words. This part of the process asks students to apply the grammatical concept to their own works, which helps them see connotation and denotation as important tools for effective writing. Before the students begin focusing on applying this concept to the pieces that they are currently writing, I remind them of the importance of making sure that the connotation and tone align. I revisit the mentor texts described in this chapter and depicted in Figure 8.3 and stress that each of these authors had a particular tone in mind when creating each of these works and chose words with connotations that aligned with that tone. Once the students start working, I hold individual conferences with them that focus on connotation and denotation. In these conferences,

I ask students to show me a word that has a specific connotation and explain why they chose that word. As the students answer, I listen carefully to make sure that they understand the connotation of the word in question and that the word's connotation aligns with the tone of the piece of writing. If students accurately explain the word's connotation and the reasons for its use, I leave the conference confident that they understand the relationship between understanding connotation and effective writing.

5. Ask Students to Reflect on the Importance of Connotation

The final step of this instructional process is to ask students to reflect on the importance of connotation. To help engage students in this reflection, I write on the board, "Why is it important that writers understand the connotations of their words?" and ask students to share their thoughts. When recently working with a group of seventh graders on this topic, I was particularly impressed by one student who explained, "If writers don't understand the connotations of their words, they could send a different message than they mean to. They could mean to say something nice, but use a word with a negative connotation by accident, and make someone mad." Another student built on this idea by making a connection to communicating outside of school: "If you write something in a text (message), and use a word that has a negative connotation and you don't know, you could really make someone mad. You have to understand connotation when writing in that way too."

Final Thoughts on Distinguishing among Connotations of Words with Similar Denotations

- Common Core Language Standard 7.5 calls for students to distinguish among the connotations of words with similar denotations.
- Connotations are the associations we make with particular words while denotations are the dictionary definitions of those words.
- An effective writer needs to understand that words with similar denotations can have very different connotations. Good writers are aware of the kind of tone that they are creating in their writing and are sure that the words they select have connotations that align with that tone.
- When teaching students about connotation and denotation:
  - Show students examples from literature of words with specific connotations and explain those connotations.

112 ◆ Grammatical Concepts Aligned with Grade 7

- Ask students to change key words in these examples so that they have different connotations.
- Ask students to create their own sentences, using words with specific connotations, and then replace those words.
- Have students work on their own writing, focusing on the connotations and denotations of their words.
- Ask students to reflect on the importance of connotation.

Figure 8.5 depicts this instructional process in an easy-to-follow flowchart.

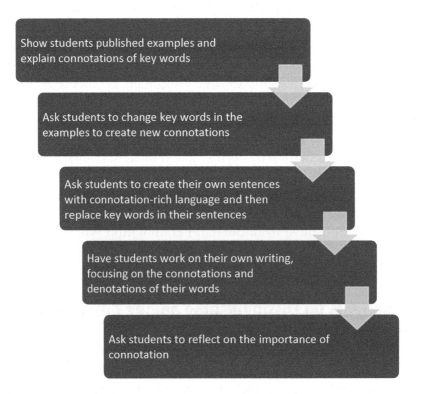

Figure 8.5 Connotations and Denotations Instructional Flowchart.

Part III

Grammatical Concepts Aligned with Grade 8 Common Core Language Standards

Introduction

In this part, we'll look closely at four grammatical concepts highlighted in the Common Core Language Standards for Grade 8. We'll begin with Chapter 9, which describes types of verbals and their impact on writing. Next, in Chapter 10, we'll think about the features and impact of the active and passive voices. After that, in Chapter 11, we'll consider a variety of verb moods, looking closely at the indicative, imperative, interrogative, conditional, and subjunctive moods. Finally, in Chapter 12, we'll reflect on how and why writers use punctuation to indicate pauses or breaks in their works. Like the chapters in Parts I and II, each of these chapters begins with an explanation of its focal concept, which is followed by a discussion of its importance to effective writing. Next, you'll find a classroom Snapshot section, in which I discuss my experiences teaching that chapter's grammatical concept to an eighth-grade English class. Following that, I'll share some essential suggestions for teaching your students about the focal topic. Each chapter concludes with some final thoughts on the importance of the concept being described and key points to remember when teaching your students about it.

The four grammatical concepts in this section represent important tools that authors use to express ideas and structure sentences in meaningful ways. By understanding and implementing all of these strategies in their works, our students can grow as strategic and metacognitive writers. For example, the verbals discussed in Chapter 9 show the flexibility of language: this chapter explains how grammatical concepts containing verb forms (such as gerunds, participles, and infinitives) do not always function as verbs in sentences—they can also be used as other parts of speech, such as nouns, adjectives, and adverbs. For example, the gerund phrase "writing poetry" allows us to create statements such as "Writing poetry is his favorite way to spend a rainy Sunday." In this sentence, "writing poetry" functions as the subject of the sentence. As we'll explore in more detail in this chapter, verbals give writers flexibility that allows them to express their ideas as clearly and accurately as possible.

We'll then continue to explore the flexible and purposeful use of language by providing important information on the features and uses of the active and passive voices in Chapter 10. In this chapter, we'll consider the ways writers strategically use both of these voices and reflect on how thinking about these concepts can help enhance students' metacognitive awareness of grammar and language. Chapter 11 then explores how "The indicative, imperative, interrogative, conditional, and subjunctive moods are important to good writing because strong writers understand that each mood must be used with a specific purpose in mind." These verb moods discussed in Chapter 11 can also develop students' understandings of authors' intentional uses of language and this will be examined in more detail in the chapter. The use of punctuation to indicate a pause or break, explored in Chapter 12, applies the strategic approach present in the section's other chapters to punctuation by looking at ways published authors use commas, ellipses, and dashes in their works to maximize their readers' experiences. Authors can utilize these punctuation tools to separate important pieces of information and ensure that readers stop briefly to pause between that information.

These chapters will give you strong understandings of the attributes of these grammatical concepts, the purposeful and strategic ways writers use them to enhance their works, and ways to teach your students about their effectiveness. Let's explore these important eighth-grade concepts!

9

Explaining the Functions of Verbals

What Are Verbals?

Common Core Language Standard 8.1 calls for students to "Explain the function of verbals (gerunds, participles, infinitives) in general and their function in particular sentences" as part of a more general statement that students must "Demonstrate command of the conventions of standard English grammar and usage when writing or speaking" (Common Core State Standards Initiative, 2010). It's important to note that this concept is an important component of effective writing regardless of a specific state's Common Core adherence: understanding gerunds, participles, and infinitives can give students developed understandings of the complexities and features of the English language.

Verbals are grammatical concepts that are formed using verbs but do not function as verbs in sentences. Instead, they function as different parts of speech, such as nouns, adjectives, or adverbs. As Common Core Standard 8.1 indicates, there are three kinds of verbals: gerunds, participles, and infinitives. Let us look at each of them in detail.

Gerunds

Gerunds are "-ing" forms of verbs, such as "running" or "reading," that function as nouns. They can appear as single words or as gerund phrases. In the sentence "Running is Sam's favorite activity," the word "running" is a gerund; it is an "-ing" form of the verb "run" and plays a noun role in this sentence. We could expand the gerund "running" in this sentence and turn it into a gerund phrase: "Running through the yard is Sam's favorite activity." In this sentence, "running through the yard" is a gerund phrase; it is an expanded form of a gerund that plays a noun role in the sentence. It is important to note that gerunds can take any role in a sentence that any other noun can take. Three roles that nouns often take in sentences are subjects, direct objects, and objects of prepositions. In the following sentence, the gerund phrase "reading outside" is the object of the preposition "by": "Julie relaxes by reading outside," while in the sentence "Julie enjoys reading outside," the gerund phrase "reading outside" is the direct object of the verb "enjoys" because it tells us what she enjoys.

Participles

Participles are verb forms that function as adjectives. As discussed in Chapter 6, there are two kinds of participles: present participles (called the "-ing" form of a verb), and past participles (called the "-en" form of a verb). Like gerunds, participles can appear as single words or as phrases. In the sentence "Smiling, the singer emerged from backstage," "smiling" is a present participle. We can expand this participle to turn it into the participial phrase "smiling at her fans," such as in the following sentence: "Smiling at her fans, the singer emerged from backstage." Now, let us examine a sentence with a past participle: "Amazed, John stared at the beautiful picture." Revised to include a participial phrase, this sentence can read: "Amazed at his sister's artistic talent, John stared at the beautiful picture."

Infinitives

Infinitives are formed by combining "to" with the base form, or present tense, of a verb (such as "to become," "to fly," or "to win"). Like gerunds and participles, infinitives can be used on their own or as part of a phrase. For example, the sentence "Josh wants to fly" contains the infinitive "to fly," while the sentence "Josh wants to fly in a hot-air balloon" contains the infinitive phrase "to fly in a hot-air balloon." Infinitives and infinitive phrases are the most versatile of all the verbals, as they can function as nouns, adjectives, or adverbs. Let us take a look at how they can function as each of these parts of speech.

Infinitives function as nouns when the action being described takes on a noun role in a sentence. In the previously mentioned sentence "Josh wants to fly in a hot-air balloon," the infinitive phrase "to fly in a hot-air balloon" is a noun; it is a thing that Josh wants. Infinitives function as adjectives when they are used to describe nouns, such as in the sentence "This is the best restaurant to eat pizza." In this sentence, the infinitive phrase "to eat pizza" functions as an adjective because it describes the noun "restaurant." Finally, let us examine how infinitives function as adverbs. Infinitives are sometimes used to provide additional detail about a previously used verb, resulting in them taking on an adverbial role. In the sentence "Chris exercised to improve his health," the infinitive phrase "to improve his health" functions as an adverb; it describes why Chris exercised. In the next section, we will take a look at why these verbals are important tools for good writing.

Why Are Verbals Important to Good Writing?

Verbals are important tools for writing because they allow writers to make their works as clear and accurate as possible. Verbals provide writers with flexibility that they would not otherwise have; without verbals, writers would only be able to use "action" words or phrases in verb roles and their abilities to clearly describe situations would be limited. In this section, we will look at gerunds, participles, and infinitives in more depth, exploring why each is important to good writing and looking at how published author Aisha Saeed uses each one in her 2018 novel *Amal Unbound*.

Gerunds

Gerunds are important tools for effective writing. Writers sometimes want to indicate that a particular action takes on a noun role in a sentence and gerunds represent a way to communicate that information clearly and accurately. The importance of gerunds to clear and accurate writing emerges in *Amal Unbound*. In this book, the narrator and protagonist Amal strongly desires to be a teacher. When describing her experiences staying after school with her favorite teacher Miss Sadia and learning from her, Amal explains "I loved watching her go over her lessons and rework them based on what worked and what didn't the day before" (p. 3). In this statement, the gerund phrase "watching her go over her lessons and rework them based on what worked and what didn't the day before" is central—it communicates exactly what Amal loved about spending time with Miss Sadia. Without the use of gerunds, author Aisha Saeed (through Amal's narration) would not be able to express the main idea of this sentence clearly. The sentence's gerund phrase helps readers understand the situation and, by extension, Amal's interests.

Participles

Participles and participial phrases can help add important details to a piece of writing, as they allow writers to include important information that helps readers clearly understand and picture a situation. For example, in *Amal Unbound*, author Aisha Saeed utilizes a participial phrase to provide descriptive information when Amal states "The sun blazed overhead, warming my chador and my hair beneath it" (p. 6). In this sentence, the participial phrase "warming my chador and my hair beneath it" allows readers to understand the situation in detail. If the participial phrase was not used, we readers would have general knowledge of the situation: we'd know about the warm sun overhead. However, when the participial phrase is used, we gain a more developed understanding: we know that Amal is wearing a chador, which is a large cloth designed to cover the head and upper body, and that the sun's heat warmed her chador and her hair. This participial phrase allows us to visualize the situation being described more clearly and understand it in more detail than if it was not used.

Infinitives

Infinitives are versatile tools, and therefore can enhance a piece of writing in a number of ways. The specific kind of impact an infinitive has on a piece of writing depends on the particular way it is used in the piece. The following example from *Amal Unbound*, in which Amal describes her goal of becoming a teacher, is an example of an infinitive phrase being used as a noun: "I wanted to be a teacher when I grew up" (p. 3). In this excerpt, the infinitive phrase "to be a teacher when I grew up" functions as a noun (specifically, the direct object of the verb "wanted"). This action accurately describes Amal's career aspiration, and Aisha Saeed uses this infinitive phrase to enable Amal to clearly express this information.

The versatility of infinitives lies in the way they can not only function as nouns, but also as adjectives and adverbs, grammatical concepts that provide additional detail to a piece of writing. The following sentence from *Amal Unbound* contains an example of an infinitive phrase being used as an adverb: "We lined up by the chalkboard at the front of the class to get our tests" (p. 2). In this sentence, the infinitive phrase "to get our tests" is used to add detail that explains why Amal and her classmates lined up by the chalkboard. This phrase plays an adverbial role in the sentence because it provides information and description of an action the characters performed. Without this infinitive phrase, the sentence would still be grammatically correct, but would not communicate all of the information it currently does.

As these examples from *Amal Unbound* combine to show, verbals are important components of good writing because they allow writers to use verb forms to express their ideas clearly and accurately. When I talk with students about the importance of verbals, I ask them to consider what challenges would emerge if verbals were eliminated and concepts such as gerunds, participles, and infinitive no longer existed. Each of the sentences from *Amal Unbound* described here would lack important information if Aisha Saeed did not use verbals in her writing. Strong writers such as Saeed use verbals to express their ideas clearly and help readers develop strong understandings of particular situations. In the next section, we will take a look at a verbal-focused activity I conducted with a class of eighth graders.

A Classroom Snapshot

If you entered the eighth-grade English classroom in which my students and I are working on verbals, you would be greeted by a cacophony of grammar-related exclamations, such as "I found a gerund!" and "This book has a ton of participles!" I have divided the students into groups of four, and each group is looking through a number of books in an attempt to find and correctly identify each of the three kinds of verbals we have discussed. Each group of students has its desks circled together and has assembled a variety of books. Students are using books from the classroom library, their lockers, and their backpacks, intently looking through them to find at least one gerund, participle, or infinitive. As students find one of each of these types of verbals, they write the sentence and the name of the book in which it was found on a chart of paper I provided (a blank version of this chart, for you to copy and use with your students, can be found in the appendix). The first group to find one of each wins.

"I see great work!" I exclaim as I walk around the room. I sit down next to the students in one group and one of its members updates me on their progress: "We found an infinitive and a participial phrase. We found an infinitive in *An Abundance of Katherines* (a 2006 novel by John Green) and a participial phrase in the story 'Push Up' (a 1993 short story by Gary Soto found in *Local News*, a book of his stories). The infinitive we found is 'to work' in the sentence 'I need to work,' and the participial phrase we found is 'lying by the floor furnace' in the sentence 'Lying by the floor furnace, the older cat had seemed more mellow and forgiving.'"

Just as I am finishing up my conversation with these students, I hear "We found all three!" called out from across the room. I hustle over to that group and take a look at their work. Sure enough, these students have found all three types of verbals. From the 1999 nonfiction work *The Freedom Writers Diary* by Erin Gruwell and The Freedom Writers, they identified the participial phrase "trying not to panic" in the sentence "Trying not to panic, I pulled my brother into my seat." From Walter Dean Myers, 1988 novel *Fallen Angels*, this group found the gerund phrase "putting you on the spot" in the sentence "'I don't like putting you on the spot,' he said." From that same book, they located the infinitive phrases "to fire my weapon" and "to destroy the nightmare around me" in the sentence "I wanted to fire my weapon, to destroy the nightmare around me."

"Fantastic job!" I respond. The rest of the class continues to work on identifying gerunds, participles, and infinitives from literature and I continue to check in with them and monitor their progress. As the period draws to a close, I notice that all of the groups have located all of the types of verbals and recorded them on their handouts. "Excellent work today—all of our groups have found all three verbal types and correctly labeled them. You all did a really nice job of finding all of these."

Recommendations for Teaching Students about Verbals

In this section, I describe a step-by-step instructional process to use when teaching students about gerunds, participles, and infinitives, the verbals described in this chapter and indicated in Common Core Language Standard 8.1. The instructional steps I recommend are: (1) show students examples of verbals in published works; (2) show students how these sentences would look without verbals, highlighting the usefulness of verbals; (3) ask students to look through published texts and label examples of verbals; (4) have students try to use each of these kinds of verbals in their own writing; and (5) ask students to reflect on the importance of verbals for effective writing. Since this process is designed to help students apply their understandings of verbals and consider their uses in effective writing, I recommend using the definitions and examples at the beginning of this chapter to ensure that students understand the fundamental components of this concept before beginning these instructional activities.

1. Show Students Examples of Verbals in Published Works

The first step of this instructional process is to show students published examples of all three kinds of verbals described in this chapter. Presenting students with mentor texts of effective verbal use can increase their familiarity with and understanding of gerunds, participles, and infinitives. I tell my middle school students (many of whom love watching television shows about animals) that looking at a published example of a grammatical concept is like seeing an animal in its natural habitat—it is sometimes easier to understand why an animal acts the way it does when seeing its behavior in nature compared to seeing it at the zoo. Since verbals can be difficult to understand, I believe it is important to show students how published authors use them. The verbals from *Amal Unbound* previously described in this chapter (and depicted in Figure 9.1) are all good examples of these concepts and a possible mentor text you might use to show your students how one published author uses all three of these types of verbals.

Passage from Novel	Verbal	Specific Type of Verbal
"I loved watching her go over her lessons and rework them based on what worked and what didn't the day before" (p. 3).	"watching her go over her lessons and rework them based on what worked and what didn't the day before"	Gerund phrase
"The sun blazed overhead, warming my chador and my hair beneath it" (p. 6).	"warming my chador and my hair beneath it"	Participial phrase
"I wanted to be a teacher when I grew up" (p. 3).	"to be a teacher when I grew up"	Infinitive phrase—functioning as a noun
"We lined up by the chalkboard at the front of the class to get our tests" (p. 2).	"to get our tests"	Infinitive phrase—functioning as an adverb

Figure 9.1 Mentor Examples of Verbals from *Amal Unbound*.

2. Show Students How These Sentences Would Look without Verbals, Highlighting the Usefulness of Verbals

After you show your students examples of effective verbal use in published texts, I recommend that you show them how these sentences would look without verbals. I have found that doing this has helped my students understand the importance of verbals to good writing. After showing my students the examples from *Amal Unbound* depicted in Figure 9.1, I will show them Figure 9.2, which contains those sentences in their original forms as well as how they appear with the verbals removed. Once you have shown your students these original and revised sentences, talk with them about what the revised versions do not tell us that the original ones do. I recommend doing this by asking students what kind of information each verbal provides and why that information is important to the sentence. Analyzing these "before and after" examples can help students to understand the importance of verbals to effective writing and the reasons why authors use them.

3. Ask Students to Look Through Published Texts and Label Examples of Verbals

After the students have examined published texts with and without verbals, the next step is to engage them even more actively in the subject by sending them on a verbal "scavenger hunt." This activity, described in this chapter's

Original Passage from Novel	Sentence with Verbal Removed
"I loved watching her go over her lessons and rework them based on what worked and what didn't the day before" (p. 3).	"I loved"
"The sun blazed overhead, warming my chador and my hair beneath it" (p. 6).	"The sun blazed overhead"
"I wanted to be a teacher when I grew up" (p. 3).	"I wanted"
"We lined up by the chalkboard at the front of the class to get our tests" (p. 2).	"We lined up by the chalkboard at the front of the class"

Figure 9.2 Sentences from *Amal Unbound* with and without Verbals.

classroom snapshot, calls for groups of students to look through any books they have available and try to find at least one example of each of the verbals identified in Common Core Language Standard 8.1: gerunds, participles, and infinitives. When I do this activity with my students, I give each group a chart (available in the appendix for you to copy and use in your classes) that asks them to write a sentence from a published text that contains one of these verbals, identify the verbal in the sentence, and state what type of verbal it is. While I make sure that all of the groups have time to finish, I also like to add a bit of competition to the activity by encouraging each group to find all three types first. If a group of students finishes before the others (as some of the students described in the classroom snapshot did), I challenge them to try to find as many additional verbals as they can. Not only does this activity engage students in an interactive way, but it also helps them practice identifying each of these kinds of verbals and distinguishing between them. "Scavenger hunts" such as this one can be a great way for students to familiarize themselves with unfamiliar and challenging grammatical concepts.

4. Have Students Try to Use Each of These Kinds of Verbals in Their Own Writing

The next step of this instructional process calls for students to apply their knowledge of verbals to their own writing by using gerunds, participles, or infinitives (or related phrases) in the pieces that they are writing. This step asks students to take even more ownership of their learning, as they must take their knowledge of verbals and apply it to their own works. After you ask your students to use these concepts in their pieces, I recommend conferring with the students individually. During these conferences, ask your students to show you examples of the verbals they have used in their writing. If a student has not yet used one of the verbal types, talk with him or her about why writers might use that particular concept. For example, if a student has not yet used a participle, have a discussion about the ways participles can add detail to a piece of writing. If a student has not yet used an infinitive, remind him or her of the ways writers use infinitives to portray actions as nouns, adjectives, and adverbs. Talking with students about the usefulness of these grammatical concepts can help them further understand the reasons writers use them and therefore enhance their abilities to use these concepts in their own writing.

5. Ask Students to Reflect on the Importance of Verbals for Effective Writing

The final step of this instructional process is to ask students to reflect on the importance of verbals for effective writing. This activity provides a strong sense of closure to this process, as it asks students to share their thoughts on how these concepts are important tools for writers to use. I recommend engaging students in a conversation about this topic by writing on the board, "Why are verbals important to good writing?" When I recently conducted such a discussion with a group of eighth graders, I was pleased with their thoughtful responses. One student explained,

> Without verbals, it would be hard to say everything you want to say. If I said, "I went to the store to buy new shoes," I would use an infinitive to say it. The infinitive tells you why I went to the store. There might be another way to say this, but it wouldn't be as easy to understand.

This student's awareness of the clarity and detail that verbals provide shows her awareness of the usefulness of this grammatical concept.

Final Thoughts on Verbals

- ◆ Verbals are included in Common Core Language Standard 8.1.
- ◆ There are three kinds of verbals: gerunds, participles, and infinitives.
- ◆ All three kinds of verbals can be expanded with modifiers. When this happens, they are called gerund, participial, or infinitive phrases:
  – Gerunds are forms of verbs, such as "running" or "reading," that function as nouns.

- Participles are verb forms that function as adjectives. There are two kinds of participles: present participles (called the "-ing" form of a verb), and past participles (called the "-en" form of a verb).
- Infinitives are formed by combining "to" with the base form, or present tense, of a verb (such as "to become," "to fly," or "to win").
♦ Verbals are important tools for writing because they allow writers to make their works as clear and accurate as possible.
♦ When teaching students about verbals:
    - Show students examples of verbals in published works.
    - Show students how these sentences would look without verbals, highlighting the usefulness of verbals.
    - Ask students to look through published texts and label examples of verbals.
    - Have students try to use each of these kinds of verbals in their own writing.
    - Ask students to reflect on the importance of verbals for effective writing.

Figure 9.3 depicts this instructional process in an easy-to-follow flowchart.

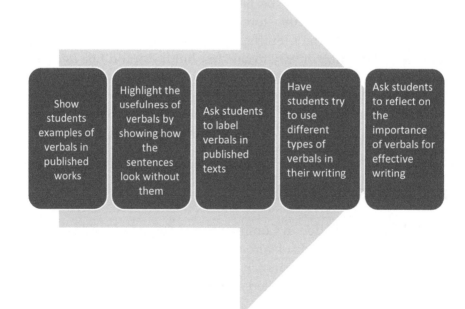

Figure 9.3 Verbals Instructional Flowchart.

10

Forming and Using Verbs in the Active and Passive Voices

What Are the Active and Passive Voices?

Common Core Language Standard 8.1 calls for students to "Form and use verbs in the active and passive voice" (Common Core State Standards Initiative, 2010) as part of a more general statement that students should demonstrate command of grammatical conventions while writing. In this chapter, we will examine what the active and passive voices are, why they are important concepts for writers to understand, and how to teach them for maximum effectiveness. Let us begin our discussion of this topic by looking at the characteristics and formation of sentences in the active and passive voices.

The Active Voice

When a sentence is written in the active voice, the subject of the sentence is performing the action (the person or thing performing the action in a sentence is sometimes called the "agent"). The sentence "Steve stole the cookies" is in the active voice. Steve is the subject and the agent, as he performed the action of stealing the cookies. In an active voice sentence, the person or thing performing the action will be placed before the verb (just as "Steve" is placed before "stole" in our example here), while the direct object follows the verb (as "the cookies" does in this example). Now, let us look at the characteristics of passive voice sentences and how this sentence changes when converted to it.

The Passive Voice

A sentence written in the passive voice is organized differently from one in the active voice. The subject in a passive voice is not the agent—it is the person or thing on which that action was performed. If we changed the active voice sentence "Steve stole the cookies" into the passive voice, the sentence would become "The cookies were stolen by Steve," making "the cookies," which was the direct object in the active voice sentence, the new subject. Kolln and Funk (2012) explain the process for converting an active voice sentence to a passive one: (1) turn the original direct object into the subject of the new sentence; (2) change the verb in the sentence into the past participle and add a form of "be" in front of it (for example, the verb "stole" in the active voice sentence changes to "were stolen" in the passive voice); and (3) if the author chooses, turn the original agent into the object of the preposition "by" or "for." This third step is optional because many passive voice sentences do not include the original subject, which creates sentences such as "The cookies were stolen," rather than "The cookies were stolen by Steve."

Why Understanding the Active and Passive Voices Is Important to Good Writing

It is important that effective writers understand the differences between the active and passive voices and when to use each of these sentence types. Many people prefer the active voice because it is more direct and clear. A sentence in the active voice clearly tells you who is performing a particular action and does not make you wait until the end of the sentence to find out. Plus, it emphasizes the person doing the action rather than the thing to which the action was done.

However, there are times when writers might want to use the passive voice instead, such as when an author wants to put more emphasis on the action completed and the thing impacted by that action than on who performed it. For example, the sentence "Next year's school calendar was approved by the principal" puts more emphasis on the fact that next year's school calendar was approved than on the fact that the principal approved it. In addition, there are times when writers may not want to say who performed an action at all. In the sentence "Mistakes were made," the writer does not tell us who made the mistakes. The passive voice provides writers with the opportunity to state that something happened without telling readers who performed that action. In this section, we will take a look at some published examples of active and passive sentences and explore why the author of each sentence may have chosen that particular sentence type.

In his 2002 novel *Things Not Seen*, which describes the experience of a teenage boy who becomes invisible, author Andrew Clements uses both the active and passive voices at times that are appropriate for their uses. In the following sentence, Clements has Bobby, the book's protagonist and narrator, describe his actions using the active voice: "I drop the fleece blanket in the living room" (p. 37). The active voice is appropriate for this sentence, as its use emphasizes Bobby's actions. If Clements used the passive voice instead, creating the sentence "The fleece blanket was dropped in the living room by me" (or "The fleece blanket was dropped in the living room," if he chose to eliminate the agent), the focus would be on the blanket instead of Bobby. Since the fleece blanket is not crucial to the novel, Clements does not focus the reader's attention towards it. Using the active voice here keeps the reader's attention directed towards Bobby.

At another point in *Things Not Seen*, Clements uses the passive voice to direct the reader's attention towards an important object. When describing a car accident in which Bobby's parents were injured, Clements includes dialogue from a television news report that discusses this crash. In this news report, the reporter uses the passive voice to focus the sentence on the car in which Bobby's parents were traveling: "As you can see, the Taurus has been pushed up onto the sidewalk by the force of multiple impacts" (p. 36). If this sentence were written in the active voice, it could read: "As you can see, multiple impacts have pushed the Taurus up onto the sidewalk." Written in the passive voice, the Taurus (the car in which Bobby's parents were traveling) takes on a more prominent role. The active sentence focuses more on the multiple impacts than the car. Since the status of the Taurus (and, by extension, Bobby's parents) is crucial to this story, it is logical that Clements would want to have the reporter use the passive voice to focus this sentence on the car.

Nonfiction writers also use the active and passive voices in their works at strategic times. In his nonfiction text *Billy the Kid: Outlaw of the Wild West*, Roger Bruns (2000) uses the active and passive voices strategically. When describing a chaotic gunfight in Lincoln, New Mexico, in which bullets filled the air from all sides, Bruns uses the passive voice to focus on the people who were shot while de-emphasizing who was actually doing the shooting. For example, in a discussion of a particularly dangerous situation in which "a maze of bullets had sprayed from all sides," Bruns writes, "Alexander McSween himself was shot down at the door" (p. 63). Bruns uses the passive voice to describe the death of McSween (a lawyer and a prominent figure in this battle) because the chaotic nature of the gunfire in which he died made it difficult to tell who actually shot him. Written this way, Bruns can state that McSween died without speculating on his killer.

At other times in this book, Bruns uses the active voice to clearly express who performed a particular action. When describing a hanging sentence given to Billy the Kid, Bruns writes, "On April 30th, 1881, Governor Lew Wallace signed Billy the Kid's death warrant" (p. 89). This sentence focuses on its agent, Governor Lew Wallace of New Mexico, and his legal action towards Billy the Kid. If Bruns rewrote this sentence in the passive voice, it would place much more emphasis on Billy the Kid's death warrant than on Lew Wallace. For example, this sentence in the passive voice could appear as "Billy the Kid's death warrant was signed by Governor Lew Wallace on April 30th, 1881" or even as "Billy the Kid's death warrant was signed on April 30th, 1881," eliminating mention of Lew Wallace entirely. We can tell from Bruns' use of the active voice that he chooses to emphasize Lew Wallace's role in this situation.

So, why is understanding the active and passive voices important to good writing? When writers understand the uses of each of these grammatical concepts, they can effectively use them as tools that can enhance their works. A good writer will use the active voice when the situation calls for it, and will do the same with the passive. The examples in this section from *Things Not Seen* and *Billy the Kid: Outlaw of the Wild West* represent authors using these sentence types strategically and in ways that are aligned with whatever aspect of a sentence they choose to emphasize. The active voice sentences discussed in this section focus on the agents described in those sentences, while the passive voice sentences strategically emphasize other elements. In the next section, we will take a look inside an eighth-grade English class and see how these students think carefully and analytically about the active and passive voices.

A Classroom Snapshot

In our past few classes, I have discussed with my eighth graders the fundamental elements of the active and passive voices, shown them published examples of each, and talked with them about how these sentences would be different if they were written in the other voice. Today, I am asking them to apply the knowledge they have gained so far in our work on this concept by creating sentences in the active voice, changing them into the passive, and commenting on the differences between those sentences.

Before the students begin this activity, I model for them what I will be asking them to do by showing them the chart depicted in Figure 10.1. This chart contains a sentence I created in the active voice, that sentence changed to the

Sentence in Active Voice	Changed to Passive Voice	Analysis of the Differences
A recent tornado damaged the town hall.	The town hall was damaged by a recent tornado.	The sentence in the active voice puts most of its emphasis on the tornado, while the sentence in the passive voice puts most of its emphasis on the town hall. If you wanted readers to pay more attention to the tornado, you would use the active voice. However, if you wanted readers to focus more on the fact that the town hall was recently damaged, you would use the passive voice.

Figure 10.1 Model of Active/Passive Voice Activity.

passive voice, and my analysis of how these sentences are different (a blank, reproducible version of this chart is available in the appendix).

I place the chart on a document camera, projecting it to the front of the classroom, and read it aloud to the students. After reading it, I explain that I would like the students to be able to share something similar with the class as part of this activity. Each group, I explain, will be responsible for orally presenting a sentence in the active voice, a version of that sentence in the passive voice, and an analysis of how they are different. "When you're coming up with your analysis," I explain, "say something about why someone might use each of these sentences, like I did in the example here. Why would someone use the active voice sentence? Why would someone use the passive voice one? I'll keep this example up here on the projector so that you can see it while you work."

I divide the students into four groups and they begin working. As they do so, I move around the room, listening to their discussions and monitoring their progress. One group has done a great job of creating a sentence in the active voice, but is having trouble converting it into the passive voice. "We're going to say 'I ate the pizza' for our active voice sentence, but we're having a hard time putting it into the passive voice," one of the group members explains. "Is it 'I was eating the pizza?'"

"Let's think about how to put it in the passive voice," I tell them. "Remember that in the active voice, the thing doing the action, which we call the agent, is the subject of the sentence, while in the active voice it isn't. What's the agent here?"

"I," one student says, "because the sentence says 'I ate the pizza.'"

"Very good," I reply. "Since 'I' is the agent and the subject of the active voice sentence, it can't be the subject of the passive voice sentence."

One student asks, "Is 'the pizza' the subject of the passive voice sentence?"

"Yes, it is. Great job," I tell her. "So, how might this sentence look in the passive voice?"

That same student answers, "It could be 'The pizza was eaten by me.'"

"Very nice," I respond. "How do you all think these two sentences are different?"

"Well," begins another student in the group, "the active voice sentence emphasizes that 'I' ate the pizza. It's like the sentence is saying that no one else can have eaten the pizza because I did it. The passive version isn't emphasizing that 'I' did it."

"Yeah," says another student, "the passive voice sentence puts more emphasis on the pizza than on who ate it. I guess the passive voice does that. It takes the emphasis away from who did the action."

"Really nicely said," I tell the group. "That was a very good analysis of the differences in the emphases of these sentences. I can't wait to hear you share your sentences and thoughts with the class."

I continue to circulate the classroom, checking in on each group and providing support to those that need it. Once all of the groups are ready, I tell the class that it is time for each of our groups to share their sentences and analyses. Student hands go up all over the room; I call on a group in the back of the classroom to begin this portion of the activity. A student from this group begins, "Our sentence in the active voice is 'Last night, Meg used the computer.' When we turned this sentence into the passive voice, we made it 'Last night, the computer was used.'"

"Very good," I reply. "A passive voice sentence can eliminate the agent entirely. Now, tell us about your analysis."

One of the students in the group explains, "The first sentence, the one in the active voice, makes it clear that Meg used the computer. Our sentence in the passive voice makes it so that no one knows who used the computer. It's mysterious," she says, smiling.

"That's a great point," I say. "A writer can use the passive voice to avoid mentioning the agent, and writers might want to do this sometimes."

After the rest of the groups also present their sentences and analyses, I address the class: "All of our groups did great work today. I'm really impressed with the ways you created sentences in the active and passive voices and analyzed the differences between them. Very nice work."

Recommendations for Teaching Students about the Active and Passive Voices

In this section, I describe a step-by-step instructional process to use when teaching students about using the active and passive voices. The instructional steps I recommend are: (1) show students published examples of the active and passive voices; (2) discuss with students how each sentence would be different if it was written in the other voice; (3) ask students to work in groups to create sentences in the active voice, change them into the passive voice, and reflect on the differences between these sentences; (4) ask students to work independently to create paragraphs that use the active voice and then rewrite those paragraphs with the active voice sentences changed to passive; and (5) have students reflect on why authors use the active and passive voices. Because this process is designed to help students think critically about the uses of the active and passive voices and why understanding them is important to good writing, I recommend using the descriptions and examples of active and passive voice sentences provided at the beginning of this chapter before beginning these instructional activities.

1. Show Students Published Examples of the Active and Passive Voices

The first step of this instructional process is to show students published examples of the active and passive voices, such as those from *Things Not Seen* and *Billy the Kid: Outlaw of the Wild West* previously discussed in this chapter. When showing students these sentences, talk with them about the focus of each one so that they can understand the differing natures of active and passive voice sentences. Help students understand that published authors use active voice sentences to focus on the agent and passive voice sentences to take the focus to another element of the sentence. If students understand this concept, they will be on their way to thinking critically about the use of the active and passive voices. Once you have shown students published examples of the active and passive voices and talked about those examples with them, it is time for the next step of this process.

2. Discuss with Students How Each Sentence Would Be Different if It Was Written in the Other Voice

The next step of this instructional process is to talk with students about how each of the published sentences you showed them in step one would be different if it was written in the other voice (such as how an active voice sentence would be different if it was written in the passive voice, and vice versa). When I do this activity with my students, I display a chart that contains published

Original Sentence	Sentence in Opposite Voice
"I drop the fleece blanket in the living room" (active voice) from *Things Not Seen*.	"The fleece blanket was dropped in the living room by me" or "The fleece blanket was dropped in the living room" (passive voice).
"As you can see, the Taurus has been pushed up onto the sidewalk by the force of multiple impacts" (passive voice) from *Things Not Seen*.	"As you can see, multiple impacts have pushed the Taurus up onto the sidewalk" (active voice).
"Alexander McSween himself was shot down at the door" (passive voice) from *Billy the Kid: Outlaw of the Wild West*.	"At the door, someone shot down Alexander McSween himself" (active voice).
"On April 30th, 1881, Governor Lew Wallace signed Billy the Kid's death warrant" (active voice) from *Billy the Kid: Outlaw of the Wild West*.	"Billy the Kid's death warrant was signed by Governor Lew Wallace on April 30th, 1881" or "Billy the Kid's death warrant was signed on April 30th, 1881" (passive voice).

Figure 10.2 Published Sentences in Their Original and Opposite Voices.

sentences in their original voices and then those sentences rewritten in their opposite voices. Figure 10.2 depicts such a chart; it contains the published excerpts from *Things Not Seen* and *Billy the Kid: Outlaw of the Wild West* previously described in this chapter and those sentences rewritten in their opposite voices. Note that one of the passive voice sentences featured here does not include an agent, so I added the agent "someone" when changing that sentence to the active voice.

After you show these sentences to your students, talk with them about how each sentence is different in its opposite voice. For example, when discussing the sentence "On April 30th, 1881, Governor Lew Wallace signed Billy the Kid's death warrant" from *Billy the Kid: Outlaw of the Wild West*, note the different emphasis when it is rewritten in the passive voice as "Billy the Kid's death warrant was signed by Governor Lew Wallace on April 30th, 1881" or as "Billy the Kid's death warrant was signed on April 30th, 1881" by pointing out to your students how the active voice sentence emphasizes Governor Lew Wallace more than either of the passive ones does. As you discuss these differences with your students, encourage them to share their ideas about how the active and passive voice versions of these sentences are different. As the students respond, you can gauge their understandings of the differences between the active and passive voices and provide any additional support that you feel is needed. Once the students are comfortable discussing the differences in these sentences, you can move on to the next step of this instructional process.

3. Ask Students to Work in Groups to Create Sentences in the Active Voice, Change Them into the Passive Voice, and Reflect on the Differences between These Sentences

The next step of this instructional process is to ask students to work together to create sentences in the active voice, change them into the passive, and reflect on the differences. The classroom snapshot section of this chapter describes one eighth-grade class' experience working on this activity. I recommend modeling this activity for your students before asking them to begin (as I did with my students). To model the activity, create a sentence and do the following: (1) show the students how it would appear in the active voice; (2) change it to the passive and show the students this version; and (3) talk with the students about the differences you observe in those sentences. Once the students begin working on the activity, check in with each group to make sure that they understand how to form sentences in both the active and passive voice. Once you have checked in with the groups and are satisfied with their progress, ask each group to share its sentences and analyses with the class. As each group shares its sentences and analyses, the rest of the class can benefit from that group's work and its ideas.

4. Ask Students to Work Independently to Create Paragraphs that Use the Active Voice and Then Rewrite Those Paragraphs with the Active Voice Sentences Changed to Passive

The fourth step of this instructional process is to ask students to work independently to create paragraphs that use the active voice and rewrite those paragraphs with the active voice sentences changed to passive. This step extends from the previous one, in which students worked in groups to create sentences in the active voice, and then changed them to the passive. I like to use this activity as an extension of the previous one because this activity requires students to write more (since students are writing paragraphs instead of sentences) and to practice this concept independently instead of in a group. This activity gives the students the extended independent practice with this grammatical concept that can help them understand it in even more depth than they did before. When conducting this activity, I tell my students that they can write a paragraph about anything they like. The only rule is that they must use the active voice when describing someone or something performing an action. After they write these paragraphs, I tell them to rewrite them with a twist; in this new paragraph, the students must try to change the active voice sentences into the passive voice. Figures 10.3 and 10.4 depict the work of a student named Sophie on this activity.

> The falcon flew through the clouds, and it landed on a crooked old tree. With its keen eyes, it spotted a rabbit. The rabbit was nibbling at a clump of yellowing grass, and did not see the bird. The hawk rested its wings for on'y a moment, and then it dove out of the sky. Startled, the rabbit looked up. The hare leapt across the ground, but it was too late. The falcon let out a shriek of success, and it rose into the air, flapping towards its nest and the shrieks of its chicks.

Figure 10.3 Paragraph with Sentences in the Active Voice.

> The clouds were flown through by the falcon, and the crooked, old tree was landed on. A rabbit was spotted by its keen eyes. A clump of yellowing grass was being nibbled by the rabbit, and the bird was not seen. The hawk's wings were rested for only a moment, and then it dove out of the sky. Startled, the rabbit looked up. The ground was leapt across by the hare, but it was too late. A shriek of success was let out by the falcon, and the air was risen into by it, flapping towards its nest and the shrieks of its chicks.

Figure 10.4 Paragraph with Sentences in the Passive Voice.

5. Have Students Reflect on Why Authors Use the Active and Passive Voices

Now that the students have done a great deal of work discussing and creating texts written in the active and passive voices, I suggest concluding this instructional process by asking students to reflect on why authors use the active and passive voices by posing the following questions to them:

- Why do authors use the active voice?
- Why do authors use the passive voice?

I like to have students first discuss these questions in small groups before they share their ideas with the class. In a recent conversation about these reflection questions, one student explained,

> I think (authors) use the active voice to make the reader pay attention to whoever's doing the action in the sentence. They use the passive voice so the reader pays more attention to something else, and less attention to whoever did the action. I think it's good to be able to use both of these, so you can make readers pay attention to what you want them to.

This comment reveals the student's awareness of why writers use both the active and passive voices. I was particularly impressed by the student's statement that writers should be able to use both the active and passive voices, as it suggests an awareness that each of these sentence types are tools that authors use purposefully based on their objectives.

During this same conversation, I asked my students to consider how the active and passive voices each play a role in the writing they do outside of school. A few students explained that most of the writing they do outside of school involves making social plans, such as the young lady who explained,

> I use text messages and Facebook to make plans with my friends. I always use the active voice because I'll say things like "I need to do some shopping" or "I want to see that movie." These things sound a lot better in the active voice. Saying "Shopping needs to be done by me" (instead of using the active voice) just wouldn't sound right to me.

Some other students in the class mentioned that they write outside of school by blogging about their favorite sports teams or commenting on internet articles about those teams. One student, who writes a blog about the

Washington Redskins football team, said that he uses both the active and passive voice at times:

> I'll use both. I might say something like "The Redskins were defeated by the Giants," which is in the passive voice, or I might say … "the Redskins' quarterback threw a game-winning touchdown," which is in the active. It depends on what I want to emphasize.

This student's comment reveals an excellent understanding of how writers purposefully choose between the active and passive voices based on the intended effects of their works.

Final Thoughts on the Active and Passive Voices

- The active and passive voices are included in Common Core Language Standard 8.1.
- When a sentence is written in the active voice, the subject of the sentence is performing the action (such as "Steve stole the cookies").
- When a sentence is written in the passive voice, the subject is not the person or thing performing the action, but rather the person or thing on which that action was performed (such as "The cookies were stolen by Steve").
- To turn an active voice sentence into a passive one:
  - Turn the original direct object into the subject of the new sentence.
  - Change the verb in the sentence into the past participle and add a form of "be" in front of it (for example, the verb "stole" in the active voice sentence changes to "were stolen" in the passive voice).
- Turn the original agent into the object of the preposition "by" or "for," if the author chooses (Kolln & Funk, 2012).
- Good writers use the active and passive voices purposefully in their works:
  - They use the active voice to focus sentences on the person or thing performing the action.
  - They use the passive voice to take the focus away from who performed the action and focus on other elements of the sentence instead, such as the thing impacted by the action.
- When teaching students about the active and passive voices:
  - Show students published examples of the active and passive voices.

- Discuss with students how each sentence would be different if it was written in the other voice.
- Ask students to work in groups to create sentences in the active voice, change them into the passive voice, and reflect on the differences between these sentences.
- Ask students to work independently to create paragraphs that use the active voice and then rewrite those paragraphs with the active voice sentences changed to passive.
- Have students reflect on why authors use the active and passive voices.

Figure 10.5 depicts this instructional process in an easy-to-follow flowchart.

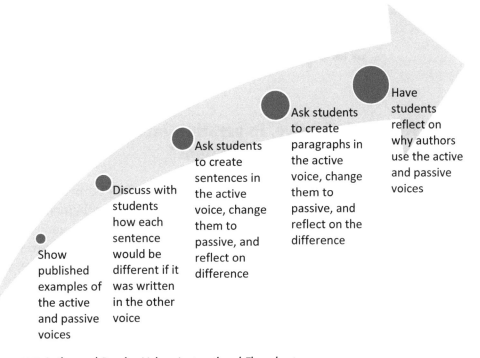

Figure 10.5 Active and Passive Voices Instructional Flowchart.

11

Forming and Using Verbs in the Indicative, Imperative, Interrogative, Conditional, and Subjunctive Moods

What Are the Indicative, Imperative, Interrogative, Conditional, and Subjunctive Moods?

Common Core Language Standard 8.1 calls for students to "Form and use verbs in the indicative, imperative, interrogative, conditional, and subjunctive mood" (Common Core State Standards Initiative, 2010) as part of a more general statement that students should demonstrate command of grammatical conventions while writing. In this chapter, we will examine what these concepts are, why they are important to good writing, and methods for teaching them.

Let us begin our exploration of this standard by first addressing what the "mood" of a verb is: according to Kolln and Funk (2012), "Mood refers to the manner in which a verb is expressed, such as a fact, a desire, a possibility, or a command" (p. 71). The concepts to which this standard refers—the indicative, imperative, interrogative, conditional, and subjunctive moods—are all possible ways for a verb to be expressed. The following subsections delve into these verb moods, providing explanations and examples of each.

The Indicative Mood
The indicative mood is one of the most straightforward of the verb moods. It is used to make a statement, such as "John plays quarterback on the football team" or "Pizza is his favorite food."

The Imperative Mood

If you are feeling bossy, the imperative mood is the one for you! The imperative mood is used to make a command. An interesting feature of sentences in the imperative mood is that the subject in these sentences is usually unstated. For example, the imperative sentences "Eat your dinner" and "Leave him alone" do not name their subjects; this information is instead understood.

The Interrogative Mood

We use the interrogative mood to ask a question. Many interrogative sentences begin with the interrogative words *why*, *where*, *when*, *who*, *what*, or *how*, such as the sentences "Who won the game?" and "Why did he do it?" but these words are not required for a sentence to be in the interrogative mood. For example, the interrogative sentence "Is he in our class?" asks a question without using any of the previously mentioned interrogative words.

The Conditional Mood

We use the conditional mood when we want to express the possibility, obligation, or necessity related to an action. When we use the conditional mood, we are not saying something will definitely happen—we are commenting on the chance that it will happen or the amount of obligation or necessity related to it happening. For example, you may want to tell a friend that you might go to his party, or perhaps you want to explain that you should clean your room this weekend. You would use the conditional mood for both of these statements, creating sentences such as "I might go to the party tonight" and "I should clean my room this weekend." Sentences in the conditional mood contain modal auxiliaries, such as *could*, *may*, *might*, *would*, and *should*, that express the level of possibility, obligation, or necessity related to an action being described.

The Subjunctive Mood

The subjunctive mood is used to express a recommendation or wish, or to describe a condition contrary to reality. This mood is used in two kinds of situations. One of these situations is in a clause, beginning with the word "that," which makes a recommendation or expresses a wish. For example, the sentence "Coach suggests that you practice your shooting" represents an example of the subjunctive mood. The clause "that you practice your shooting" begins with "that" and makes a recommendation.

The second situation in which the subjunctive is used is in a clause, beginning with the word "if," which describes a condition contrary to reality. For example, the sentence "If I didn't have to study, I would go to the concert" is an example of the subjunctive. The clause "If I didn't have to study" begins with "if" and expresses a situation contrary to reality. Similarly, the sentence "If I were you, I would stay home" is an example of the subjunctive because of its use of the clause "If I were you."

Figure 11.1 summarizes key information about the verb moods described in this section.

Mood	Explanation	Example
Indicative	The indicative mood is used to make a statement.	John plays quarterback on the football team.
Imperative	The imperative mood is used to make a command. The subject in an imperative sentence is usually unstated.	Eat your dinner.
Interrogative	The interrogative mood is used to ask a question.	Who won the game?
Conditional	The conditional mood is used to express some condition of possibility, obligation, or necessity. Sentences in the conditional mood contain modal auxiliaries, such as *could*, *may*, *might*, *would*, and *should*, to express the level of possibility, obligation, or necessity related to action being described.	I might go to the party.
Subjunctive	The subjunctive mood is used to express a recommendation or wish, or to describe a condition contrary to reality. This mood is used in two kinds of situations: (1) in a clause beginning with the word "that," which makes a recommendation; and (2) in a clause beginning with the word "if," which describes a situation contrary to reality.	(1) Coach suggests that you practice your shooting. (2) If I didn't have to study, I would go to the concert.

Figure 11.1 Explanations and Examples of Verb Moods.

Why Are Indicative, Imperative, Interrogative, Conditional, and Subjunctive Moods Important to Good Writing?

The indicative, imperative, interrogative, conditional, and subjunctive moods are important to good writing because strong writers understand that each mood must be used with a specific purpose in mind. If an author uses a mood that does not align with its intended purpose, the text will not achieve its desired result. Good writers know exactly which mood to use and why to use it. For example, a writer using an imperative sentence should understand the strong impact of this sentence type and use it only in a situation in which that effect is desired. Similarly, a writer would only use a conditional sentence when describing some condition of possibility, obligation, or necessity related to an action taking place.

In this section, we will examine how published author Nikki Grimes uses each of these moods in her 2002 novel *Bronx Masquerade*. As we will see in these examples, Grimes uses each mood purposefully and with a clear understanding of how it relates to the message being conveyed at that point in the novel. Let us look at each of these examples individually.

The Indicative Mood in *Bronx Masquerade*

One instance in which Nikki Grimes uses the indicative mood in *Bronx Masquerade* is in the sentence "I've been drawing pictures all my life" (p. 20). This sentence, told from the point of view of an artistic student named Raul Ramirez, illustrates his commitment to his art in a straightforward way. This is a good example of a purposefully used sentence mood. Grimes has Raul use the indicative mood to clearly express his level of artistic experience; no other mood would communicate this information as well.

The Imperative Mood in *Bronx Masquerade*

Nikki Grimes strategically uses the imperative mood in *Bronx Masquerade* when writing from the perspective of Devon Hope, a talented basketball player who also wants to be acknowledged as a poetry enthusiast. Devon's statement "Don't call me Jump Shot" (p. 32) makes a command. Like many other imperative sentences, it does not name the person to whom it is addressed. This sentence is effective because it strongly expresses Devon's desire to be referred to as more than a basketball player. If it was written in the indicative mood (perhaps as "I don't want people to call me Jump Shot") or in the interrogative mood ("Will you please not call me Jump Shot?"), the sentence would not communicate this sentiment as strongly.

The Interrogative Mood in *Bronx Masquerade*

Grimes uses the interrogative mood in *Bronx Masquerade* to express questions asked by characters in the novel. For example, a conversation between two characters named Leslie and Lupe includes the interrogative sentence "Lupe, what's wrong?" (p. 66). This sentence conveys Leslie's desire to know what is bothering Lupe and concern for her. If Grimes did not have Leslie use an interrogative sentence at this point in the conversation, it would be difficult for Leslie to learn more about the situation. She could say, "Lupe, I want to know what's wrong," but phrasing this sentence in the form of a question is more concise and suggests that Leslie is thoughtful and concerned, while the alternate phrasing could be construed as demanding.

The Conditional Mood in *Bronx Masquerade*

Nikki Grimes uses the conditional mood when writing from the point of view of Wesley "Bad Boy" Boone, who makes the following comment about Tyrone: "Tyrone might convince everyone else he's all through with dreaming, but I know he wants to be a big hip-hop star" (p. 3). The opening part of this sentence contains an example of the conditional mood; Wesley's statement that "Tyrone might convince everyone else he's all through with dreaming" uses the modal auxiliary "might" to express the possibility of this action taking place. Since this statement expresses the possibility related to an action, it is an example of the conditional mood. The use of the conditional mood here indicates that Wesley does not know for sure whether or not Tyrone has convinced "everyone else he's all through with dreaming." This mood allows for Wesley to acknowledge this possibility without saying for certain whether or not it has happened.

The Subjunctive Mood in *Bronx Masquerade*

The subjunctive mood expresses a recommendation or wish, or describes a condition contrary to reality. Grimes strategically utilizes this mood in *Bronx Masquerade* when expressing Tyrone's point of view about Devon's basketball skills. Tyrone's statement "If I had moves like Devon, I'd be cruising crosscourt with Scottie Pippin!" (p. 33) is a great example of the subjunctive because it uses the clause "If I had moves like Devon" to describe a condition contrary to reality. Tyrone explains to us that he does not have moves like Devon, but, if he did, he would be playing basketball with NBA great Scottie Pippin. This sentence's use of the subjunctive mood allows for Tyrone to clearly describe a condition contrary to reality, and what he would do if that scenario came true.

All five of these moods are grammatical tools used purposefully and effectively by Nikki Grimes in *Bronx Masquerade*. As these examples and the explanations of them illustrate, Grimes knew exactly what message she wanted to convey to the reader when composing each of these sentences, and chose moods that align with those messages. Figure 11.2 contains the examples from *Bronx Masquerade* described in this section and their corresponding moods.

Now, let us take a look inside a classroom and see how a group of eighth graders and I worked with the indicative, imperative, interrogative, conditional, and subjunctive moods.

Mood	Example
Indicative	"I've been drawing pictures all my life" (p. 20).
Imperative	"Don't call me Jump Shot" (p. 32).
Interrogative	"Lupe, what's wrong?" (p. 66).
Conditional	"Tyrone might convince everyone else he's all through with dreaming, but I know he wants to be a big hip-hop star" (p. 3).
Subjunctive	"If I had moves like Devon, I'd be cruising crosscourt with Scottie Pippin!" (p. 33).

Figure 11.2 Examples of Verb Modes in Nikki Grimes' Novel *Bronx Masquerade*.

A Classroom Snapshot

My eighth graders have entered the classroom, taken their seats, and completed their beginning-of-class routine, so I call them together and introduce our plan for the day: "Today, we're going to do some more work with verb moods. You've been doing a great job so far with this concept. In today's class, you're going to get a bit more active with it. My goal for this activity is that you understand verb moods even more, while also having some fun."

In today's class, I am dividing the students into groups and asking each group to change an existing sentence into a new version of that sentence that represents a different mood. I begin this activity by writing on the board, "I am going to English class" and then explaining to the students how the activity will work: "Okay, everyone, do you see the sentence written up here?" The students nod and I continue: "As you can see, this sentence reads, 'I am going to English class.' Can someone tell us the mood of this sentence?"

Student hands go up around the room. I call on a young lady who says, "It's indicative."

"You're absolutely right," I reply. "This sentence is in the indicative mood. Today, we're going to get into groups and each group is going to change this sentence. One group will change it to the imperative mood, one group will change it to the interrogative, one group will change it to the conditional, and yet another group will change it to the subjunctive. I'm going to divide you into four groups. Once you're in those groups, each group will—without looking—pull a piece of paper out of the bag I have here. There are four pieces of paper—one for each mood. If you draw the paper with imperative, you'll change the sentence to the imperative. If you draw the paper with interrogative, you'll change it to the interrogative, and the same way for the other sentence moods. You can make whatever changes to the sentence you think you need to in order to turn it into the mood your group draws. Your group's tasks are as follows: first, change the sentence to whatever mood you draw. Second, talk with your group members about how the original indicative sentence and your new version in a different mood are different from each other. Third, share your work with the class. When you share with the class, you'll tell us your new sentence, the mood of that sentence, and how that sentence is different from the original sentence, 'I am going to English class.'"

I divide the students into four groups and have a member of each group draw a piece of paper that tells the group members what mood they will be changing the original sentence to. Once all of the students have this information, they begin working on the activity, discussing with their group members how to change the original sentence to a different mood. I circulate around the room, checking in with each group. First, I sit down next to the group that chose the imperative mood and ask them how they are progressing: "How are you all doing changing this sentence to the imperative?"

"We're doing great," one student says. "We have our new sentence, and we even have a fun a way to act out saying it."

"Awesome," I reply. "Let's check it out."

One student, using a gruff voice, points at one of his group members and says, "Go to English class."

"I love it!" I exclaim. "You did a great job of turning that indicative sentence into an imperative one. I love the acting part too! Now, a question for you: how do you think this imperative sentence is different from the original indicative one?"

"Well," responds one of the group members, "one way is that the imperative sentence commands someone else to do something. The indicative sentence doesn't command someone. It just makes a statement."

"And," another student interjects, "these sentences also have different tones. The imperative one has a harsh, strong tone. The indicative has a regular tone."

"Excellent responses, both of you," I reply. "Your responses show a really nice understanding of the differences in these moods. I like your points

Mood	Sentence
Imperative	Go to English class.
Interrogative	Are you going to English class?
Conditional	I might go to English class.
Subjunctive	If I were you, I would go to English class.

Figure 11.3 Sentence Moods Shared by Students.

about the tones of the sentence and about the way one mood commands while the other states."

I continue to move around the room, checking in with all of the other groups. Once the groups have completed their work, I tell the students that it is time to share their work with the class. I remind them that each group is going to tell the class the new sentence that the group created, the mood of that sentence, and how that sentence is different from the original sentence "I am going to English class." The groups share their sentences, identify their moods, and explain the differences between the sentences they created and the original indicative sentence. The sentences all four groups created are found in Figure 11.3.

Recommendations for Teaching Students to Use the Indicative, Imperative, Interrogative, Conditional, and Subjunctive Moods

In this section, I describe a step-by-step instructional process to use when teaching students to use the indicative, imperative, interrogative, conditional, and subjunctive moods. The instructional steps I recommend are: (1) show students published examples of verb moods and discuss the reasons the author used each one; (2) ask students to change an existing sentence to a different mood and describe the differences; (3) have students find and analyze examples of verb moods in literature; (4) ask students to apply these concepts to their own writing; and (5) ask students to reflect on the importance of verb moods. Since this instructional process is designed to help students think analytically about verb moods and apply their understandings of this concept, I recommend using the information from the beginning of this chapter, such as the explanations in the chapter's opening section and the examples in Figure 11.1, to make sure students understand the fundamentals of verb moods before beginning these instructional activities.

1. Show Students Published Examples of Verb Moods and Discuss the Reasons the Author Used Each One

The first step of this instructional process is to show students published examples of verb moods and discuss with them the reasons the author of each example used each mood. This allows students to see the five verb moods used authentically in a piece of writing and facilitates discussions of why authors would use each of these moods. When conducting this activity with students, I begin by showing them a published example of a sentence written in the indicative mood, such as the previously discussed example from *Bronx Masquerade*: "I've been drawing pictures all my life" (p. 20). I tell the students that this is an example of an indicative sentence and think aloud about why an author might use it. For example, during one of these think alouds, I will say,

> This sentence makes a clear and straightforward statement. It doesn't include any commands, ask any questions, express any probability, or talk about things that are contrary to fact. Authors might use other moods to do these other things I just mentioned, but here the author makes a straightforward statement, so she uses the indicative mood. None of the other moods would get this point across as well as this mood does.

I will then continue to do this with other published examples. When showing the students the imperative sentence "Don't call me Jump Shot" (p. 32), I will explain,

> The author of this sentence used the imperative mood to show the character making a command. The imperative mood is very strong and used when one expresses a command. No other mood would get this message across as strongly, so this mood is the best fit for what the character wants to express.

When conducting this activity, you can use the five sentences from *Bronx Masquerade* depicted in Figure 11.2, or you can choose examples from a different text if you believe another author's work would be a better fit for your students. I recommend showing students examples of all five moods from one book so that you can discuss how a particular author uses all of these moods purposefully and for specific reasons. Pointing this out to students can help them understand the "grammar toolkit" metaphor, as it illustrates that each mood is a tool used for a particular purpose.

2. Ask Students to Change an Existing Sentence to a Different Mood and Describe the Differences

The next step of this instructional process is to give students a sentence and ask them to change it to a different mood and then describe the differences between the original sentence and the new version. An example of this activity is described in this chapter's classroom snapshot. As illustrated in that description, I like to conduct this activity by presenting the whole class with a sentence in the indicative mood (I used "I am going to English class" in the activity described in the classroom snapshot), dividing the students into four groups, and asking each group to change the sentence into one of the other moods. I suggest randomly assigning the mood to which each group changes the original indicative sentence by writing the words "Imperative," "Interrogative," "Conditional," and "Subjunctive" on pieces of paper, placing those papers in a bag, and having each group select one without looking. Once groups have done this, inform the students that they will need to change the indicative example to a sentence in the new mood and explain how the sentence in the indicative mood differs from the new version that they created. After the students do this, ask the groups to share with the class the new sentence they created, the mood of that sentence, and how that sentence differs from the original one. This activity requires the students to take an active role in their learning by creating and analyzing sentences and sharing those creations and analyses with the rest of the class. Once the students have completed it and you are satisfied with their understandings, it is time to move on to the next activity.

3. Have Students Find and Analyze Examples of Verb Moods in Literature

The third step is this instructional process is to have students find and analyze examples of verb moods in literature. In this activity, students continue to work in groups, looking through published texts and taking note of verb moods they find. I begin this activity by taking a number of books from the classroom library, dividing them into stacks, and giving each group of students a stack of books to use. Once the students have these books, I tell them that their task is to find at least three different verb moods in the books, identify those moods, and explain why each author used each mood. To facilitate their work, I give each group a chart that asks them to identify three sentences, the moods of those sentences, and why the author of each sentence used that mood (a reproducible version of this chart is available in the appendix).

If one group finds three verb moods in their books before the other groups have completed their work, I give that group another copy of this and challenge them to find the other two moods as well. I have found that differentiating the activity in this way keeps the faster working groups engaged while also ensuring the groups that work at slower paces are not rushed. Before the students get started on this activity, I like to show them a model so that they have a clear understanding of what to do. Figure 11.4 depicts a model of the chart that I have shown my students. It includes three sentences from Jacqueline Woodson's 2000 novel *Miracle's Boys*, the moods of those sentences, and thoughts on why Woodson used each mood in each situation.

Once the students have completed this activity, I like to ask each group to share its work with the class by telling the other students the sentences that they found, the moods of those sentences, and their analysis of why the

Sentence	Mood	Why You Think the Author Used this Method
"You thinking about Mama?" *Miracle's Boys*, p. 28.	Interrogative	Jacqueline Woodson, the author of this book, has a character use the interrogative mood here because that character is asking a question. In this situation, two brothers named Lafayette and Ty'ree are spending time together and Lafayette asks Ty'ree if he misses their mother who has passed away.
"I lay back on my bed and listened to my brother Newcharlie talking," *Miracle's Boys*, p. 1.	Indicative	Woodson (through Lafayette's narration) uses the indicative mood to describe this information in a straightforward way. No other mood would express this fact as clearly.
"Charlie, don't cry. Please don't cry," *Miracle's Boys*, p. 41.	Imperative	In this situation, Lafayette is urging his brother not to cry. He uses the imperative mood to make this urging as strong as possible. If Woodson had Lafayette use another sentence type, this message would not be as strongly worded.

Figure 11.4 Model of Verb Mood in Literature Chart.

author of each sentence used that particular mood. Sharing this work out loud allows the students to hear a variety of examples of verb moods from literature, which further illustrates the connection between this grammatical concept and effective writing.

4. Ask Students to Apply These Concepts to Their Own Writing

The next step of this instructional process is to ask students to apply all five of the verb moods to their own writing. I recommend reminding students of the uses and characteristics of each of the verb moods and then conferencing with them individually as they work to use all of these concepts in the pieces they are writing at the time. When conferencing with the students, ask them to show you some of the different verb moods they have used and to explain why they used that particular mood in that situation. The explanations students give about why they used each mood are especially important, as they illustrate the students' thought processes and understandings of the uses of these concepts. If there are any moods the students have not yet used, talk with the students about why writers use those moods and how those moods might fit into that piece. For example, if some students have not yet used a sentence in the conditional mood, ask them why a writer would use this mood. Once the students answer this question, talk with them about possible ways the pieces they are writing might be enhanced by that mood.

5. Ask Students to Reflect on the Importance of Verb Moods

The final step of this instructional process is to ask students to reflect on the importance of understanding and purposefully using verb moods. To facilitate this reflection, I recommend posting the following questions on the board and asking students to discuss them in small groups:

- ◆ Why is it important that writers understand all of the verb moods?
- ◆ How can using the correct verb mood impact a piece of writing?

After the students have discussed these questions in small groups, I ask volunteers to share their thoughts with the whole class. During a recent discussion of these questions, one eighth grader explained,

If you don't use the correct mood, your writing won't be as good. Like, if you want to tell someone what to do, you need to use the imperative. If you don't, your writing won't be as good because you didn't use the mood that goes with what you're saying.

This response reveals this student's awareness of the relationship between verb moods and effective writing. As this student suggests, using verb moods that align with a particular message allows authors to make their points as effectively as possible.

Final Thoughts on Forming and Using Verbs in the Indicative, Imperative, Interrogative, Conditional, and Subjunctive Moods

- Common Core Language Standard 8.1 calls for students to "Form and use verbs in the indicative, imperative, interrogative, conditional, and subjunctive mood" (Common Core State Standards Initiative, 2010).
- Below are explanations of each of these five verb moods:
  - The indicative mood is used to make a statement.
  - The imperative mood is used to make a command.
  - The interrogative mood is used to ask a question.
  - The conditional mood is used to express some condition of possibility, obligation, or necessity. Sentences in the conditional mood contain modal auxiliaries, such as *could, may, might, would*, and *should*.
  - The subjunctive mood is used to express a recommendation or wish, or to describe a condition contrary to reality.
- The indicative, imperative, interrogative, conditional, and subjunctive moods are important to good writing because strong writers understand that each mood must be used with a specific purpose in mind.
- When teaching students to form and use the indicative, imperative, interrogative, conditional, and subjunctive moods:
  - Show students published examples of verb moods and discuss the reasons that the author used each type.
  - Ask students to change an existing sentence to a different mood and describe the differences.
  - Have students find and analyze examples of verb moods in literature.
  - Ask students to apply these concepts to their own writing.
  - Ask students to reflect on the importance of verb moods.

Forming and Using Verbs ◆ 151

Figure 11.5 depicts this instructional process in an easy-to-follow flowchart.

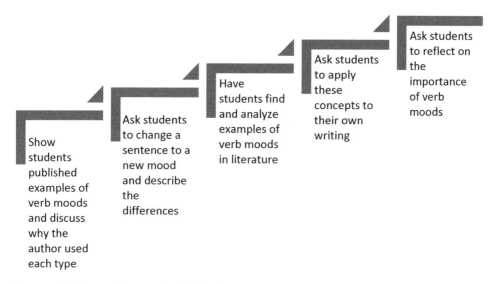

Figure 11.5 Verb Mood Instructional Flowchart.

12

Using Punctuation to Indicate a Pause or Break

What Does It Mean to Use Punctuation to Indicate a Pause or Break?

Common Core Language Standard 8.2 calls for students to "Use punctuation (comma, ellipsis, dash) to indicate a pause or break" as part of a more general statement that students need to "Demonstrate command of the conventions of standard English capitalization, punctuation, and spelling when writing" (Common Core State Standards Initiative, 2010). As this standard indicates, commas, ellipses, and dashes are forms of punctuation used to indicate a pause or break in a sentence. Regardless of a specific state's adherence to the Common Core, the use of punctuation for this purpose is a key aspect of effective writing: it allows authors to make their works as clear and impactful as possible. Let us begin our exploration of this standard by considering what it means to use punctuation to indicate a pause or break.

When writers want their readers to briefly stop and pause, they use punctuation marks—such as commas, dashes, and ellipses—to indicate this. These punctuation marks are used to separate pieces of information from each other and to tell readers to take a quick break because new information is coming. For example, I might say, "After the game, I watched a movie." Notice how the comma separates "After the game" from the rest of this sentence. This comma tells the reader to pause between two major pieces of information in the sentence—the phrase "after the game" and the independent clause "I watched a movie." Now, let us take a look at a sentence that utilizes a dash for this purpose. In the sentence "I saw Mrs. Smith—the teacher who lives on my street," the phrase "the teacher who lives on my street," which identifies Mrs. Smith, is set off from the rest of the sentence. The dash not only separates this phrase from the remainder of the sentence—it also tells readers to pause when they reach it. Finally, let us take a look at a sentence that uses an ellipsis to tell the reader to pause between separate pieces of information. In the sentence "She studied for the math test all night ... and then again the next morning," the ellipsis separates two statements that make up the sentence and tells readers to pause between them. It lets readers know that new information is coming after the first part of the sentence and that they should stop briefly before continuing to the rest of the sentence. Figure 12.1 provides an overview of the examples discussed in this section.

Why Using Punctuation to Indicate a Pause or Break Is Important to Good Writing

The use of punctuation such as commas, dashes, and ellipses to indicate a pause or break is an important part of effective writing. If a writer failed to use one of these punctuation marks in a situation that required it, readers would have difficulty making sense of the author's work. For example, if the dash was omitted from the sentence "I saw Mrs. Smith—the teacher who

Punctuation Type	Example	Explanation
Comma	After the game, I watched a movie.	The comma in this sentence tells readers to pause between "after the game" and "I watched a movie."
Dash	I saw Mrs. Smith—the teacher who lives on my street.	The dash tells readers to pause between "Mrs. Smith" and the identifying information following her name.
Ellipsis	She studies for the math test all night ... and then again the next morning.	The ellipsis in this sentence separates two statements and tells readers to pause between them.

Figure 12.1 Sentences with Commas, Dashes, and Ellipses.

lives on my street," it would read, "I saw Mrs. Smith the teacher who lives on my street." Written without the dash, this sentence is much harder to read, as readers no longer benefit from the punctuation mark that separates key sections of the sentence and indicates a pause between them. This dash provides a sense of order to this sentence that does not exist when it is omitted. Similarly, the sentence "After the game, I watched a movie" is much easier to read and understand in its original form than if the comma was removed and the sentence became "After the game I watched a movie." This comma separates important pieces of information in this sentence and ensures that readers stop briefly to pause between these pieces of information.

In this section, we will look at how Trevor Noah uses commas, dashes, and ellipses in his 2019 book *It's Trevor Noah: Born a Crime. Stories from a South African Childhood. Adapted for Young Readers.* In addition, we will consider how these sentences would look if they did not use these punctuation marks for these purposes and discuss how Noah's punctuation choices contribute to the sentences' effectiveness. First, let us take a look at a sentence from this book that uses a comma to indicate a pause and separate pieces of information. While discussing the Zulu tribe of South Africa, Noah explains, "When the colonial armies invaded, the Zulu charged into battle with nothing but spears and shields against men with guns" (p. 3). The comma following "invaded" is important to the effectiveness of this sentence because it tells the reader to pause after the introductory dependent clause "When the colonial armies invaded." By using this comma, Noah separates this information from the sentence's independent clause, "the Zulu charged into battle with nothing but spears and shields against men with guns," and tells the reader to pause between these sentence components. If there were no comma and the sentence instead read, "When the colonial armies invaded the Zulu charged into battle with nothing but spears and shields against men with guns," readers would not be told to pause between these pieces of information, making the sentence harder to understand.

Trevor Noah also uses dashes to indicate pauses or breaks in this text. For example, in the book's opening line, Noah writes "Apartheid—the South African government policy of racial segregation—was genius at convincing people who were the overwhelming majority to turn on each other" (p. 3). This sentence, which begins to introduce the injustices and effects of apartheid, contains dashes that separate the phrase "the South African government policy of racial segregation" from the rest of the sentence and indicates pauses before and after the phrase appears. These dashes help us readers understand and accurately read the sentence. If it were instead written, "Apartheid the South African government policy of racial segregation was genius at convincing people who were the overwhelming majority to turn on each other," the sentence would be much more difficult to decipher. Readers would not know to pause before and after the phrase "the South African government policy of racial segregation," and may not be able to accurately understand the information in the sentence. By using dashes before and after this phrase, Trevor Noah facilitates readers' understandings of this sentence.

Finally, let us take a look at a strategically used ellipsis in Trevor Noah's text. Noah explains that individuals of different cultures who share the same language can feel a connection that has the potential to overcome racism and prejudice, stating,

> If the person who doesn't look like you speaks like you, your brain short-circuits: the racism code of "if he doesn't look like me he isn't like me" suddenly smashes against the language code of "if he speaks like me he…is like me".
>
> (p. 50)

When crafting this statement, Noah uses an ellipsis between the components of the "language code" that he describes, creating the phrasing "if he speaks like me he…is like me." This ellipsis causes the reader to pause between "he" and "is like me"; this pause creates separation between the components of Noah's statement and places extra emphasis on the point that the individuals are alike even though they look different. Without this ellipsis, the statement would express the same basic information as it would with it, but it would not have the same impact: the ellipsis creates a pause that places extra stress on the latter part of the sentence. By using this ellipsis strategically, Noah ensures that the reader will pay extra attention to the key information in the sentence.

These examples from *It's Trevor Noah: Born a Crime. Stories from a South African Childhood. Adapted for Young Readers* convey the importance of punctuation used to indicate a pause or break to effective writing. The commas, dashes, and ellipses that Noah employs in this piece impact readers' experiences in purposeful and strategic ways. The comma highlighted in the first excerpt described in this section separates key components of a sentence by indicating where the initial dependent clause ends and where the independent clause that follows it begins. The dashes in the second play a similar role by separating parts of the sentence and signaling to readers to pause between those components. The ellipsis in the third example also communicates to readers to pause between pieces of information—this pause, between "he" and "is like me," is used strategically to emphasize the author's point. If Trevor Noah did not use these punctuation elements, his work would not have the same clarity and impact that it does. Now that we've looked at a text that purposefully utilizes these grammatical concepts, we'll examine how some eighth graders enhance their understandings of it.

A Classroom Snapshot

My eighth graders and I are in our third day discussing the grammatical concept of using punctuation marks such as commas, dashes, and ellipses to indicate pauses or breaks in writing. In our first day, I presented a mini-lesson on the topic, explaining that writers use these punctuation marks to separate pieces of information and to ensure that readers stop briefly between those pieces of information. The students and I discussed the punctuation and sentences discussed in Figure 12.1, focusing on the reasons why each of those sentences uses a comma, a dash, or an ellipsis to clarify its meaning and make the sentences as easy as possible to read. On the second day, I showed the students the sentences discussed in the previous section from Trevor Noah's book, talking with them about the punctuation used to indicate a pause or break.

In today's class, we are going to follow up on the previous day's discussion of excerpts from Noah's work: we will be using the same sentences, but this time examining how they look without the punctuation marks that indicate that readers should pause briefly while reading. I introduce the activity to the students by first displaying the three sentences from *It's Trevor Noah: Born a Crime. Stories from a South African Childhood. Adapted for Young Readers* discussed in the previous class. I remind students that we recently discussed these sentences and talk with them about the fact that all of the sentences use punctuation to communicate that the reader should pause at a designated time.

I explain that we will spend the day's class further exploring this idea by thinking about the impact that this punctuation has on the sentences from Trevor Noah's book that we previously examined. To do this, I tell the students, we will look at the original version of each sentence and a revised version of it that no longer contains the punctuation Noah uses to indicate a pause or break. I begin this conversation by displaying Figure 12.2, which depicts each of the previously discussed sentences as well as revised versions of those sentences written without key punctuation used to indicate a pause or break.

"Now," I tell the students, "we're going to break into three expert groups. Each group will be the expert on one of these sentence pairs. You'll work with your group members to analyze your sentences and think about the importance of the punctuation in the original version that indicates a pause or break. When it's time for your group to present, you'll read both versions of your sentence and then talk to the rest of us about why the punctuation in the original sentence that indicates a pause or break is important to the sentence's effectiveness. In other words, you'll tell us why this punctuation makes the sentence better."

I divide the class into groups and give each group one of the sentence pairs. "I'm very excited to hear your insight and analysis," I tell the class. As the groups discuss and analyze their sentences, I check in with each group,

Original Sentence	Sentence without Key Punctuation
"When the colonial armies invaded, the Zulu charged into battle with nothing but spears and shields against men with guns" (p. 3).	"When the colonial armies invaded the Zulu charged into battle with nothing but spears and shields against men with guns."
"Apartheid—the South African government policy of racial segregation—was genius at convincing people who were the overwhelming majority to turn on each other" (p. 3).	"Apartheid the South African government policy of racial segregation was genius at convincing people who were the overwhelming majority to turn on each other."
"If the person who doesn't look like you speaks like you, your brain short-circuits: the racism code of 'if he doesn't look like me he isn't like me' suddenly smashes against the language code of 'if he speaks like me he…is like me'" (p. 50).	"If the person who doesn't look like you speaks like you, your brain short-circuits: the racism code of 'if he doesn't look like me he isn't like me' suddenly smashes against the language code of 'if he speaks like me he is like me.'"

Figure 12.2 Sentences from *It's Trevor Noah: Born a Crime. Stories from a South African Childhood. Adapted for Young Readers* with and without Key Punctuation.

answering their questions and providing needed support. Once all of the groups have finished their conversations and are ready to present, I ask the first group to share its insights with the rest of the class. A student from the group reads the sentence "When the colonial armies invaded, the Zulu charged into battle with nothing but spears and shields against men with guns," pausing at the comma between "invaded" and "the." Then, another student in the group rereads the sentence without pausing at this point in the sentence. The group concludes by discussing the importance of the comma to the sentence's effectiveness, explaining that the sentence became much harder to understand without the pause that the comma creates. "It was really hard to tell where one part of the sentence ends and the other begins," explains one student in the group. "Without the comma, it all just blends together."

After the first group shares its ideas, the second group, which analyzed the sentence "Apartheid—the South African government policy of racial segregation—was genius at convincing people who were the overwhelming majority to turn on each other" (p. 3) presents its insights. The first student to read pauses at the dashes that separate "the South African government policy of racial segregation" from the rest of the sentence, while the second student, who reads the revised version without commas, does not. After these strong readings, the group members comment on the importance of these dashes to the sentence's effectiveness, noting that they are important tools for clarity in the sentence. One student explains that the dashes are especially significant to readers' abilities to understand the sentence "because they show that the part of the sentence that says 'the South African government policy of racial segregation' is additional detail that describes apartheid. Without the dashes," the student tells the class, "it's way harder to figure that out."

Finally, the third group shares its ideas and expertise. A student begins by reading the sentence

> If the person who doesn't look like you speaks like you, your brain short-circuits: the racism code of "if he doesn't look like me he isn't like me" suddenly smashes against the language code of "if he speaks like me he…is like me"

(p. 50)

pausing carefully and emphatically at the ellipsis. Next, another student reads the sentence without the pause indicated by the ellipsis. Following these readings, the group discusses the importance of the ellipsis to the effectiveness of the first sentence; one group member explains, "This ellipsis makes us pause at an important part of the sentence. When we pause there, we put extra emphasis on what comes afterwards." Another student in the group interjects, "Yeah, it's like when your parents tell you to clean your room now and they pause before 'now' to really emphasize that part of the sentence. The author is doing the same kind of thing here. He's using the ellipsis and pause to emphasize the part of the sentence that says 'is like me.'"

Once all of the groups have shared, I praise the students' work: "I'm so impressed with how well you all did today. You read the sentences carefully and shared very insightful points about the importance to the original text of the punctuation that indicates a pause or break. Very nice job!"

Recommendations for Teaching Students to Use Punctuation to Indicate a Pause or Break

In this section, I describe a step-by-step instructional process to use when teaching students to use punctuation (such as commas, ellipses, or dashes) to indicate a pause or break. The instructional steps I recommend are: (1) show students published examples of sentences that use punctuation to indicate a pause or break; (2) show students revised versions of those examples with key punctuation omitted and discuss the differences; (3) ask students to find examples from literature that use punctuation to indicate a pause or break and analyze those examples; (4) ask students to apply this concept to their writing; and (5) have students reflect on why using punctuation to indicate a pause or break is important to effective writing. Because these steps are designed to help students consider the importance of using punctuation to indicate a pause or break, I recommend using the information at the beginning of this chapter, such as the examples and explanations described in Figure 12.1, to ensure that students understand the fundamentals of this concept before proceeding to these steps.

1. Show Students Published Examples of Sentences that Use Punctuation to Indicate a Pause or Break

The first step in this instructional process is to show students examples of published sentences that use punctuation to indicate a pause or break. This initial step shows students the importance of this concept to published works. When I do this activity with students, I begin by showing them published sentences that use punctuation marks such as commas, ellipses, or dashes to indicate a pause or break in the sentence. After I present these examples to students, I identify the punctuation marks that the author uses to tell the reader to pause while reading. When doing this activity with my eighth graders, I used the three examples from the Trevor Noah book described in this chapter. While discussing the sentence "When the colonial armies invaded, the Zulu charged into battle with nothing but spears and shields against men with guns" (p. 3), I identified the comma between "invaded" and "the," pointing out that Trevor Noah uses this comma to tell readers that they need to pause between the dependent and independent clause while reading this sentence. After identifying related types of punctuation in the other two sentences, I transitioned to the next activity, which asks students to compare these original sentences with revised versions that do not contain key punctuation marks.

2. Show Students Revised Versions of Those Examples with Key Punctuation Omitted and Discuss the Differences

The next step of this instructional practice is to show students revised versions, with key punctuation omitted, of the sentences used in step one and then discuss with them the differences between these new versions and the original ones. My work with a group of eighth graders on this activity is described in this chapter's classroom snapshot section, in which my students performed this task with key sentences from *It's Trevor Noah: Born a Crime. Stories from a South African Childhood. Adapted for Young Readers* in which the author purposefully uses punctuation to indicate a pause or break. I recommend beginning this activity with a chart such as the one depicted in

Figure 12.2, which contains the original versions of published sentences and those sentences without key punctuation that tells readers to pause or break while reading. Once you show students these sentences, have volunteers read them out loud and hold a class discussion of how the originally punctuated version of each sentence differs from its revised version.

This activity is especially useful because of the way it clearly illustrates the importance of the punctuation marks that tell readers to pause or break in the middle of a sentence. Instead of simply telling students to use commas, ellipses, and dashes, this activity shows students how ineffective and confusing a piece of writing would be if it did not use these grammatical concepts. Once students have examined and discussed published sentences in their original forms and in alternate versions that do not use punctuation to indicate a pause or break, they will have a deeper understanding of why this grammatical concept is important to high-quality writing.

3. Ask Students to Find Examples from Literature that Use Punctuation to Indicate a Pause or Break and Analyze Those Examples

Now that you have shown students published examples of sentences that use punctuation to indicate a pause and discussed how those sentences would differ without those punctuation marks, it is time to have your students take an even more active role in this process. To do so, I recommend asking students to find examples from literature that use punctuation to indicate a pause or break and then analyze those examples. I suggest having the students work in small groups and look through books from the classroom and/or school library, with the goal of finding sentences that use a comma, a dash, or an ellipsis to indicate a pause or break in the sentence. I recommend asking the students to find at least two sentences—each with a different punctuation mark used to indicate a pause in the sentence.

In addition, I like to ask the students to analyze each sentence they find by explaining why the comma, dash, or ellipsis is important to the sentence. If some students find two such sentences quickly, I ask them to look for the form of punctuation they have yet to find or more examples of the ones they have already found. To guide the students through this activity, I give them a chart that asks them to record two sentences they find that use punctuation to indicate a pause or break, the kind of punctuation used for that purpose, and why they believe that punctuation is important to the sentence (a reproducible version of this chart for you to use is available in the appendix).

Before students begin this activity, I suggest showing them a model of a completed chart and explaining it. Doing this ensures that the students understand how to fill out their own charts and allows you to think aloud about the choices you made when completing your own version. Figure 12.3 depicts a model of the chart used in this activity that I have shown my students before

Sentences you Found that Use Punctuation to Indicate a Pause or Break	Type of Punctuation Used for this Purpose	Why this Punctuation is Important to the Sentence
"If he's turned into a Nazi—which is very likely—I'll just turn around," *The Book Thief*, p. 125.	Dashes	These dashes are important to the sentence because they tell the reader to pause before and after reading "which is very likely." The dashes set "which is very likely" apart from the rest of the sentence.
"When it came to stealing, Liesel and Rudy first stuck with the idea that there was safety in numbers," *The Book Thief*, p. 272.	Comma	The comma in this sentence is important because it tells the reader to pause between "stealing" and "Liesel." This comma separates "when it came to stealing" from the rest of the sentence.

Figure 12.3 Model of Chart to Use when Finding Examples from Literature of Punctuation that Indicate a Pause or Break.

asking them to complete their own. This model chart contains two sentences from Markus Zusak's (2005) novel *The Book Thief*. Once the students have completed their work on this activity, I recommend asking each small group to share its work with the class. If you have access to a document camera, I suggest having each group place its work on that camera so that the sentences they copied down are visible to the whole class. This allows the other students to see the punctuation in the sentences as the different groups share and analyze them.

4. Ask Students to Apply This Concept to Their Writing

The fourth step in this instructional process is to ask students to apply the concept of using commas, dashes, or ellipses to indicate a pause or break to their own writing. At this point of the instructional process, the students have looked at a number of literary examples of this concept and are ready to try it out on their own. To get students started on this activity, I tell them to work on the pieces they are currently writing and try to use all three punctuation forms we have discussed (commas, dashes, and ellipses) to indicate pauses or breaks in the piece. As the students do so, I hold individual conferences with them and ask them to show me ways that they have used these punctuation marks to indicate pauses or breaks in their writing. Each time a student shows me an example, I ask him or her to also explain to me why it is important that this punctuation mark is included. For example, a student recently showed me a sentence in which she had inserted a dash to indicate that the reader should pause. When I asked her why that dash was important, she explained, "If it wasn't there, you'd just keep reading without stopping. (The dash) makes sure you pause between the different parts of the sentence."

5. Have Students Reflect on Why Using Punctuation to Indicate a Pause or Break Is Important to Effective Writing

The final step of this instructional process involves asking students to reflect on the importance of this concept to effective writing. When students consider why it is important to use punctuation to indicate a pause or break, they also think about the relationship between this grammatical concept and good writing. As with any element of grammar, it is important that students think of this concept as a tool that writers use to enhance their works and not just something to be memorized or applied to a workbook exercise. To facilitate this reflection, I will ask students to discuss the following questions in small groups:

- Why is it important that writers use punctuation marks such as commas, ellipses, and dashes when they write to indicate a pause or break?
- What might happen if they failed to do so?

After the students have discussed these questions in small groups, I will ask for volunteers to share their reflections with the whole class. During a recent discussion, one eighth grader explained, "If you were writing something and you didn't use one of these punctuation marks to tell your reader to pause, the reader would think everything was one big statement instead of a sentence made up of different statements." This response struck me as especially insightful because of the awareness it demonstrates of how commas, ellipses, and dashes divide sentences into "different statements." Writers use these punctuation marks to tell readers to pause or break between statements, making their works as clear and easy to understand as possible.

Final Thoughts on Using Punctuation to Indicate a Pause or Break

- Common Core Language Standard 8.2 calls for students to "Use punctuation (comma, ellipsis, dash) to indicate a pause or break" (Common Core State Standards Initiative, 2010).

- ◆ These punctuation marks are used to separate pieces of information from each other and to tell readers to take a quick break because new information is coming.
- ◆ The use of commas, dashes, and ellipses to indicate a pause or break is an important part of effective writing because it can separate key elements of a sentence and ensure a clear understanding for the reader.
- ◆ When teaching students about using punctuation to indicate a pause or break:
  - Show students published examples of sentences that use punctuation to indicate a pause or break.
  - Show students revised versions of those examples with key punctuation omitted and discuss the differences.
  - Ask students to find examples from literature that use punctuation to indicate a pause or break and analyze those examples.
  - Ask students to apply this concept to their writing.
  - Have students reflect on why using punctuation to indicate a pause or break is important to effective writing.

Figure 12.4 depicts this instructional process in an easy-to-follow flowchart.

Step One	Step Two	Step Three	Step Four	Step Five
Show students published examples of punctuation that indicate a pause or break	Show revised versions without key punctuation and discuss differences	Ask students to find and analyse examples from literature of punctuation used in these ways	Ask students to apply this concept to their writing	Have students reflect on why using punctuation to indicate a pause or break is important to effective writing

Figure 12.4 Punctuation to Indicate a Pause or Break Flowchart.

Part IV

Putting It Together

13

Assessing Students' Knowledge

In this chapter, we will discuss one of the greatest challenges associated with grammar instruction: the issue of assessment. Research reveals that worksheets and out-of-context tests are ineffective methods of assessing students' knowledge of grammatical concepts because they do not actually measure students' abilities to use these concepts in their writing (Weaver, 1998), which presents the question: how do teachers assess their students' grammatical knowledge in authentic ways? I have fielded questions about this topic when presenting at conferences and talking with teachers about grammar instruction. Many times, I have been asked questions along the lines of, "Everything you're saying about grammatical concepts being tools for good writing sounds great, but how can I assess if my students have learned the material?" I believe this is an excellent question and one that needs to be further explored. To that end, this chapter addresses ways to assess students' knowledge of the grammatical concepts described in this book and addressed in the Common Core Language Standards.

In this chapter, I describe two types of summative assessments to use when evaluating students' understandings of grammatical concepts. After discussing these assessment methods and ways to put them into practice as summative assessments, I address ways to also use them as formative assessments (in-process assessments that can be used to informally monitor students' progress). The two types of assessment methods described in this chapter are: (1) a student-created analysis of a published text; and (2) a student-created exemplar of a grammatical concept and corresponding analysis. These assessment methods provide students with ways of applying their understandings of the grammatical concepts discussed in this book; instead of simply reciting facts, students are called to use their knowledge of particular grammatical concepts to comment on the importance of those concepts to effective writing. The assessment methods described here are designed to provide teachers with useful information about how well their students understand specific grammatical concepts and how those concepts are important tools for effective writing. Let us take a look at each of these assessment methods in more detail.

Assessment Method One: Student-Created Analysis of a Published Text

The first assessment method we will discuss is a student-created analysis of a published text. In this method of assessment, students find a published example of the grammatical concept on which you are assessing them and analyze why that concept is important to that piece of writing. This assessment method requires students to read a published work critically and with an awareness of how a particular grammatical concept is important for the effectiveness of this piece. I let my students choose the text that they would like to use for this activity, as long as it is a generally grade-level appropriate fiction or nonfiction book that incorporates the focal concept. For example, when conducting a summative assessment on sixth graders' understandings of intensive pronouns, I give them the assignment sheet depicted in Figure 13.1.

This assignment sheet notifies students that they will need to identify and analyze an author's use of intensive pronouns in a piece of writing. While this particular example focuses on intensive pronouns, this assignment can be adapted to focus on the other grammatical concepts described in this book. For example, I have asked sixth graders to conduct analyses of how an author uses punctuation to set off nonrestrictive elements. In their analyses, the students found situations where published authors use punctuation to set off nonrestrictive elements from the rest of a sentence and then wrote essays discussing why the author did this and how the text being analyzed would be different if the author had not used punctuation to set off nonrestrictive elements. No matter what grammatical concept is being analyzed, the benefits of this assessment method remain consistent: (1) students look carefully for an example of a grammatical concept in a published text; and (2) students think critically about how that grammatical concept enhances the piece of writing. To evaluate students' work on this assessment, I use the rubric depicted in Figure 13.2.

This rubric contains two areas of evaluation: the accuracy of information included in the student work and the quality of the analysis. I assess each of these areas separately because I see them as progressive elements in the students' thinking. First, they need to accurately identify the concept on which they are being assessed. After they have done this, they can engage in detailed and thoughtful analysis of it.

Assignment Sheet: Intensive Pronoun Published Text Analysis

Great job on your work so far with intensive pronouns! This assignment sheet describes your next task related to this concept. For this task, you'll conduct an analysis of the intensive pronouns used in a piece of writing. To complete this task, you'll need to do the following things:

- Look through some published books until you find one that you believe uses an intensive pronoun effectively. Identify one example of an intensive pronoun that you believe is especially effective. (Any fiction or nonfiction book that is written on approximately a sixth-grade level can work for this activity. Ask me if you have questions about a specific book.)

- Write an essay that analyzes how the author of your book uses this intensive pronoun. In this essay, you'll need to quote directly from the book you're using and analyze why the author of this book chose to use an intensive pronoun in this situation. To complete this analysis, ask yourself why the author chose to use this intensive pronoun and how this piece of writing would be different if the author chose not to use it.

Figure 13.1 Sample Assignment Sheet for Published Text Analysis.

Area of Evaluation	Evaluation Questions	Possible Points	Your Score
Accuracy of information	Have you correctly identified an example of the focal concept? Is it clear that you have an excellent understanding of this grammatical concept?	5	
Quality of analysis	Is the analysis of the concept detailed? Does this analysis show an excellent understanding of how this grammatical concept is important to the piece of writing you selected?	5	

Total score:

Comments:

Figure 13.2 Rubric for Analysis of Published Text.

Assessment Method Two: Student-Created Exemplar of a Grammatical Concept and Corresponding Analysis

In addition to the previously described assessment method, I like to evaluate students' knowledge of grammatical concepts by asking them to create a piece of writing that purposefully uses a specific grammatical concept and then reflect on how that grammatical concept is important to the piece they created. I recommend combining this assessment with the previous one so that students are completing two different assessment tasks on each concept. Assessment method two requires students to create their own works and then analyze how a particular grammatical concept impacts those works, and, like assessment method one, can be used to evaluate students' understandings of any of the grammatical concepts described in this book. When using this method to conduct a summative assessment of students' knowledge of intensive pronouns, I give them the assignment sheet depicted in Figure 13.3.

Assignment Sheet: Student-Created Exemplar and Analysis of Intensive Pronouns

In this assignment, you'll create a piece of writing that uses intensive pronouns and then analyze why those intensive pronouns are important to the piece of writing that you created. You won't be analyzing a published text like you did for the first assessment; this time, you'll be creating your own work and then analyzing it. You'll be responsible for the writing *and* the analysis!

To complete this task, you'll need to do the following things:

- Create an original piece of writing about any topic you like—fiction or nonfiction! It should be about one paragraph long.

- In this piece of writing, use two examples of intensive pronouns. Be sure to underline them. This piece is called the exemplar because you'll be creating an excellent example of a piece of writing that uses this grammatical concept.

- After you've finished this, write an essay in which you analyze your use of intensive pronouns. In this essay, you'll need to quote directly from your piece and analyze how the intensive pronouns you used enhanced the work you created. To complete this analysis, ask yourself how your work would differ if it did not include the intensive pronouns that it does.

Figure 13.3 Sample Assignment Sheet for Student-Created Exemplar and Analysis of a Grammatical Concept.

When I introduce this assignment to my students, I emphasize that they are free to choose the topic of the exemplar they create. If student have difficulty coming up with a topic, I encourage them to write about their interests. I have had students do great work on this activity writing about television shows, sports, and outings with friends and family. Since middle schoolers value the way writing allows them to share their thoughts about high-interest topics (Robb, 2010), encouraging students to write about their interests for this assessment can enhance their engagement. To evaluate students' work on this activity, I use the rubric depicted in Figure 13.4.

Like the rubric used for assessment method one, this rubric evaluates the accuracy of information in the students' work and the quality of the analysis. Since the task associated with this assessment practice differs from the task in the first assessment practice, the evaluation questions differ somewhat as well. For example, this rubric asks if each student has used three examples of the focal concept. In addition, instead of asking if the student's analysis

Area of Evaluation	Evaluation Questions	Possible Points	Your Score
Accuracy of information	Does your exemplar correctly use two examples of the focal concept? Does your analysis correctly identify the examples of the focal concept you used? Is it clear that you have an excellent understanding of this grammatical concept?	5	
Quality of analysis	Is the analysis of the concept detailed? Does this analysis show an excellent understanding of how this grammatical concept is important to the piece of writing you created?	5	

Total score:
Comments:

Figure 13.4 Rubric for Student-Created Exemplar and Analysis of a Grammatical Concept.

shows an excellent understanding of the importance of the grammatical concept to the piece the student selected (as the previous rubric does), this rubric asks a similar question about the piece the student *created*.

How to Use These Assessment Methods as Summative Assessments

After you and your students have completed the instructional activities described in this book for a particular concept, I recommend using the two assessment methods discussed in this chapter as summative assessments that evaluate their understandings. For example, after you and your students have completed the instructional process outlined in Chapter 1 that focuses on teaching students to use intensive pronouns, assess their learning through the assessment methods described in this chapter. Ask them to find a piece of published writing that uses this concept and analyze it, and then ask them to create their own piece that incorporates these concepts and analyze that work as well. Use the rubrics included in this chapter to evaluate their work. Each response can earn up to ten points using this rubric, producing a maximum score of 20 points.

How to Use These Assessment Methods as Formative Assessments

The two assessment methods described in this chapter can also be used as formative assessments, which are informal assessments that can be used throughout a unit of study to monitor students' understandings. When using these assessment practices as formative assessments, I adjust their length and requirements and ask students to complete them as "exit questions" (short responses that students complete at the end of a class period).

When using assessment method one as a formative assessment, I will write on the board for students to find an example from a published text of the grammatical concept we are discussing and to briefly explain why they think that the writer chose to use it. For example, when using this assessment practice to conduct a formative assessment of students' knowledge of intensive pronouns, I will write on the board: "Find an example of an intensive pronoun from one of the books in our classroom. Write down the sentence in which it is found and explain why you think the author used it."

These directions are similar to the ones I give students when they are completing this task as a summative assessment, but the context is different. Instead of grading these exit questions, I respond with comments that highlight what they have done well and call attention to any parts that might be incorrect or need further explanation. If any students' exit questions indicate that they are struggling with a concept, I will revisit this concept with individual instruction, a small-group mini-lesson, or a whole-class review (depending on how many students are having trouble).

When using assessment method two as a formative assessment, I will conduct a similar activity by presenting the students with an exit question related to this assessment practice. When using this assessment practice to conduct a formative assessment of students' knowledge of intensive pronouns, I will write on the board: "Write a sentence that uses an intensive pronoun. Underline the intensive pronoun and briefly explain its important to the sentence."

Just like I do when using assessment method one as a formative assessment, I will respond to my students' work with comments that highlight strengths and call attention to elements that are incorrect or could be further explained. I will use these formative assessments to determine how well my students have grasped this concept and if there are any elements we should review before moving forward.

Using These Assessments to Guide Future Instruction

It is important to note that both the formative and summative assessment methods described here are useful for guiding future instruction. The summative assessments tell teachers how well the students have grasped specific concepts at the end of a unit of study, while the formative assessments provide information on how well the students are understanding certain concepts while that unit is in progress. Using the formative assessments throughout the learning process can alert you to the students' developing understandings and tell you what aspects of a concept to review or focus on in more depth. While the summative assessments allow you to evaluate students' understandings at the end of a unit, remember that instruction on a concept does not end when a summative assessment is administered. Use the summative assessment results to provide any extra support and review to students who need it so that all students can eventually demonstrate mastery of these important grammar tools.

Final Thoughts on Assessing Students' Knowledge

- I recommend assessing students' knowledge of the grammatical concepts described in this book in two different ways: (1) a student-created analysis of a published text; and (2) a student-created exemplar of a grammatical concept and corresponding analysis.
- In the student-created analysis of a published text, students find published examples of the grammatical concept on which you are assessing them and analyze why that concept is important to that piece of writing.
- In the student-created exemplar of a grammatical concept and corresponding analysis, students create pieces of writing that purposefully use a specific grammatical concept and then reflect on how that grammatical concept is important to the pieces they created.
- The assessment methods described in this chapter can be used as both summative and formative assessments:
  - When using these assessments as summative assessments, ask your students to complete them after you and your students have finished working on a particular grammatical concept.
  - When using these assessments as formative assessments, I adjust their length and requirements and ask students to complete them as "exit questions" (short responses that students complete at the end of a class period).
- It is important to note that both the formative and summative assessment methods described here are useful for guiding future instruction:
  - The summative assessments tell teachers how well the students have grasped specific concepts at the end of a unit of study.
  - The formative assessments provide information on how well the students understand certain concepts while that unit is in progress.

Conclusion

Final Thoughts and Tips for Classroom Practice

Think back to the vignette that opens up the introductory chapter of this book, in which I described the importance of grammar to my students by telling them, "Grammatical concepts are like tools writers use to make their writing more descriptive, clear, or interesting, just like a marker or paintbrush is a tool an artist can use to add more color to a picture." I used this vignette to frame the ideas and activities described in this book, which are designed to help middle school students think about grammar in insightful and meaningful ways; specifically, as tools for effective writing rather than as out-of-context facts to be quickly learned and then forgotten. Given the emphasis that the Common Core Standards and other rigorous state standards place on grammatical concepts, I believe it is especially important that middle school teachers teach their students language standards in a way that improves the students' writing and enhances their awareness of how writers use specific grammatical concepts to make their pieces as strong as possible. The Common Core Language Standards for Middle School, as well as other rigorous state standards, address challenging and important grammatical concepts, and understanding these concepts can inform students' knowledge of good writing and help them carry this knowledge well into the future.

In this chapter, we will take a look at some especially important tips for putting the ideas in this book into practice. These recommendations, which are rooted in the idea that grammatical concepts are important tools for effective writing, are:

- ◆ Discuss the fundamental components of a grammatical concept.
- ◆ Show students examples of this concept in published texts.

- Discuss with students why the grammatical concept is important to the published examples you have shown them.
- Have students work in small groups to analyze the importance of a grammatical concept.
- Have students apply a specific grammatical concept to their own writing.
- Ask students to reflect on the importance of a grammatical concept to effective writing.

Now, let us take a look at each of these ideas in more detail.

Recommendation One: Discuss the Fundamental Components of a Grammatical Concept

Before students begin thinking about how published authors use a specific grammatical concept and why it is important to effective writing, they must understand the fundamentals of that concept. Each of the chapters in this book that focuses on a specific grammatical concept contains important fundamental information about that concept. For example, Chapter 5, which focuses on simple, compound, complex, and compound-complex sentences, contains definitions, examples, and explanations of each of these sentence types. When teaching any of the grammatical concepts discussed in this book, use the information at the beginning of that concept's chapter to introduce students to the fundamental components of that concept and the key pieces of information related to it. Once your students are comfortable with this information, you can challenge them to think in more depth about the concept and how it is an important aspect of effective writing.

Recommendation Two: Show Students Examples of This Concept in Published Texts

After the students have developed an understanding of the fundamentals of a particular grammatical concept, it is time to show them examples from published texts of this grammatical concept. When students see published examples of a grammatical concept, they can begin to understand that elements of grammar are not simply things to be learned in isolation and used on worksheets; they are integral aspects of quality writing. Each of the chapters in this book contains examples of published works that use the grammatical concept on which that chapter focuses. While the examples discussed in this book are strong ones that you can certainly use with your students, I also recommend keeping your own students' interests and reading levels in mind when selecting examples to show them. As I mention in the introduction to this book, I ask myself three questions when selecting a published example of a particular grammatical concept to show my students: (1) Does this example clearly illustrate the grammatical concept I want my students to learn? (2) Is this example from a text that is age-and reading-level appropriate for my students? (3) Do I believe my students will be interested in this example? If I answer "yes" to all three of these questions, then I know the mentor text is one I will use.

Recommendation Three: Discuss with Students Why the Grammatical Concept Is Important to the Published Examples You Have Shown Them

Once you have shown students examples of published texts that contain a particular grammatical concept, the next step is to talk with them about why that grammatical concept is important to those particular texts. While the specific nature of these conversations will vary based on the concept you are describing, the main focus will remain the same: why the grammatical concept being discussed is important to the piece of writing. For example, a conversation about the active voice will differ from a discussion about using punctuation to set off a nonrestrictive element, but each conversation should address the importance of the concept being described and help students reflect on its importance. When having these discussions with students, I recommend focusing on two key questions: (1) Why did the author use this grammatical concept? (2) What would this piece of writing be like if this concept was not used? These questions help students consider how grammatical concepts are tools that writers use purposefully to improve their works.

Recommendation Four: Have Students Work in Small Groups to Analyze the Importance of a Grammatical Concept

Now that you have talked with students about why a particular grammatical concept is important to a piece of writing, the next step is to ask students to work together in small groups and further analyze the importance of that concept. This step is related to the gradual release of responsibility method of instruction (Pearson & Gallagher, 1983) described in the introduction to this book, which asks students to take more ownership of their learning as instruction progresses. At this point in your instruction, you have taught students the fundamental components of a grammatical concept, shown them examples from published texts of that concept, and have talked with them about why that concept is important to those published works. Now the students are ready to take more of an active role in their learning by working in small groups to think further about the importance of a grammatical concept.

There are different ways for students to work collaboratively to analyze the importance of a grammatical concept, and you will find a number of variations on this activity described in the book based on the nature of the focal concept. For example, published texts do not often appear with dangling modifiers in them, so I do not ask students to find examples of dangling modifiers in books they are reading. Instead, I give them sentences as they originally appeared in published works and revised versions of those sentences that include dangling modifiers and then ask the students to analyze how the dangling modifiers change the meaning of the sentences. In contrast, when working on pronoun case, I will ask students to find examples of different pronoun cases in literature and explain why the author of that piece used that particular case. I recommend looking through the individual chapters of this book to find different variations on this activity that are specific to the concept being taught. The most important elements of this activity are that students are taking increased ownership for their learning and are working together to analyze the importance of the grammatical concept that they are studying. After students complete their small group analysis, I recommend having them share their ideas with the whole class so that all can benefit from each group's work on the concept.

Recommendation Five: Have Students Apply a Specific Grammatical Concept to Their Own Writing

After students have worked in groups on a specific grammatical concept, the next step is to ask them to individually apply that same concept to their writings. This activity places even more responsibility on the students, as it requires that they work independently to use the focal grammatical concept in their writings. If students are already working on a particular piece of writing, you can ask them to apply the grammatical concept you are focusing on to that piece. For example, if the class is studying specific nouns and strong verbs (grammatical concepts described in Chapter 7 of this book), you can ask the students to focus on applying these concepts as they continue to work on their pieces. While your students work on using a specific grammatical concept, hold individual writing conferences with them in which you talk with them about the ways that they are using the concept. These conferences are great opportunities to ask students to show you examples of this concept in their work, talk with students about its importance, and clarify any confusion students have.

Recommendation Six: Ask Students to Reflect on the Importance of a Grammatical Concept to Effective Writing

The final step of this process is to ask students to reflect on the importance of a particular grammatical concept to effective writing. Doing so further encourages students to think about the significance and relevance of grammar. I recommend engaging students in this kind of reflection by placing a question on the board that asks them why a grammatical concept is important to good writing and having the students discuss this question in small groups and then with the whole class. For example, when working with my seventh graders on connotation (as described in Chapter 8), I posed the question: "Why is it important that writers understand the connotations of their words?" The students reflected on this concept, with one pointing out that accidentally using a word with a negative connotation could upset a reader. When asking students to reflect on the importance of a grammatical concept, I encourage you to help students to make connections to the writing that they do outside of school. These kinds of connections can make a particular concept even more relevant. For example, one student, when describing the importance of connotation, pointed out that it is important to understand the connotations of particular words when using them in text messages. This student's comment shows an understanding of this grammatical concept and an awareness of how it relates to middle school students' everyday lives.

Final Thoughts on the Middle School Grammar Toolkit

The grammatical concepts described in this book represent more than key elements of the Common Core Language Standards for the sixth, seventh, and eighth grades: they also represent important tools that writers use to enhance their works in thoughtful and specific ways. The updates to this new edition combine with the core ideas that are conveyed from the original version to give you a resource on grammar instruction designed to be as useful and relevant as possible. The flowcharts in Chapters 1 through 12 are resources that can help you visualize the instructional processes described in each chapter and easily enact them in your classroom. If you need a reminder of what teaching students about the book's focal grammatical concepts can look like, you can return to the book's streamlined classroom snapshots, which are structured to focus on the key aspects of the described instruction. This book is firmly rooted in the importance of mentor texts and authentic, literature-based examples of grammatical concepts; with this in mind, I suggest using the published examples throughout the chapters and in the annotated bibliography. Since this edition contains more contemporary texts from a wider and more diverse range of authors, you'll have a number of current examples to use with your students that provide a variety of important perspectives.

In addition, the information in this edition about the changing nature of pronoun use highlights important ideas for us all to consider related to the evolution of language and the importance of inclusivity of all gender identities. Also, with regard to the book's title change from *The Common Core Grammar Toolkit: Using Mentor Texts to Teach the Language Standards in Grades 6–8* to *The Middle School Grammar Toolkit: Using Mentor Texts to Teach Standards-Based Language and Grammar in Grades 6–8, Second Edition*, it's important to emphasize that the grammatical concepts discussed in this book are essential tools for effective writing regardless of whether or not one's specific state adheres to the Common Core Standards. No matter your state's connection to those standards, the book you have just finished reading will give you a toolkit of actionable takeaways and ideas designed to facilitate your teaching and your students' learning.

As you work with your students on the concepts described in this book, I recommend instilling in them that all of these concepts are key parts of writers' toolkits. An understanding of each of these tools will help today's middle school students develop into thoughtful readers and writers who understand that grammar is more than a series of workbook exercises: it is a key element of how writers communicate effectively. Students who understand this can read and write with an awareness of why writers do what they do, and contribute to the world with their strong communication skills.

Annotated Bibliography

This annotated bibliography contains the following information: (1) the titles and authors of the works of young adult literature that I describe in this book as exemplars of particular grammatical concepts; (2) a key grammatical concept found in each work; (3) the Common Core Standard connected with that concept; (4) an excerpt from that work, found earlier in this book, that demonstrates exactly how the author uses that grammatical concept; and (5) information on the chapter of this book in which the concept is discussed (in case you want to refer back to the text for more information on a concept).

The annotated bibliography is designed to make this book as user-friendly as possible. It is organized alphabetically by author's last name and each entry includes important details designed to help you use literature to teach these grammatical concepts.

Avi (1990). *The true confessions of Charlotte Doyle.* New York, NY: Harper Trophy.
Title: *The True Confessions of Charlotte Doyle*
Author: Avi
Grammatical Concept: Intensive pronoun use
Related Common Core Standard: L6.1
Excerpt that Demonstrates Concept:
"If I wanted to wash things—and I did try—I had to do it myself" (p. 67).
Discussed in Chapter: 1

Berman, L. (2009). *The greatest moments in sports.* Naperville, IL: Sourcebooks Jabberwocky.
Title: *The Greatest Moments in Sports*
Author: Len Berman
Grammatical Concept: Intensive pronoun use
Related Common Core Standard: L6.1
Excerpt that Demonstrates Concept:
"The crowd went wild. One of those on his feet was Howe himself" (p. 29).
Discussed in Chapter: 1

Brooks, B. (1994). *Predator.* New York, NY: Farrar, Straus, & Giroux.
Title: *Predator*
Author: Bruce Brooks
Grammatical Concept: Connotation
Related Common Core Standard: L7.5
Excerpts that Demonstrate Concept:
"Not that you ever doubted your superior strength, or your speed, or your craftiness" (p. 29).
"It is easy to see that many predatory animals are smart" (p. 13).
Discussed in Chapter: 8

Bruns, R. (2000). *Billy the Kid: Outlaw of the Wild West.* Berkeley Heights, NJ: Enslow.
Title: *Billy the Kid: Outlaw of the Wild West*
Author: Roger Bruns
Grammatical Concept: Passive voice
Related Common Core Standard: L8.1
Excerpt that Demonstrates Concept:
"Alexander McSween himself was shot down at the door" (p. 63).
Discussed in Chapter: 10
Another Grammatical Concept in this Text: Active voice
Related Common Core Standard: L8.1
Excerpt that Demonstrates Concept:
"On April 30th, 1881, Governor Lew Wallace signed Billy the Kid's death warrant" (p. 89).
Discussed in Chapter: 10

Cartaya, P. (2017). *The epic fail of Arturo Zamora.* New York, NY: Puffin Books.
Title: *The Epic Fail of Arturo Zamora*
Author: Pablo Cartaya
Grammatical concept: Using phrases and clauses while recognizing and correcting dangling modifiers
Related Common Core Standard: L7.1
Excerpts that Demonstrate Concept:
"'That's right,' I said, wishing she didn't have such a good memory" (p. 16).
"My mom walked over to the couple, said hello, and then turned to walk away, smiling uncomfortably as she tried to get Abuela to follow her" (p. 27).
Discussed in Chapter: 6

Clements, A. (2002). *Things not seen.* New York, NY: Puffin Books.
Title: *Things Not Seen*
Author: Andrew Clements
Grammatical Concept: Active voice
Related Common Core Standard: L8.1
Excerpt that Demonstrates Concept:
"I drop the fleece blanket in the living room" (p. 37).
Discussed in Chapter: 10
Another Grammatical Concept in this Text: Passive voice
Related Common Core Standard: L8.1
Excerpt that Demonstrates Concept:
"As you can see, the Taurus has been pushed up onto the sidewalk by the force of multiple impacts" (p. 36).
Discussed in Chapter: 10

Collins, S. (2008). *The hunger games.* New York, NY: Scholastic.
Title: *The Hunger Games*
Author: Suzanne Collins
Grammatical Concept: Eliminating wordiness through strong verb use
Related Common Core Standard: L7.3
Excerpts that Demonstrate Concept:
"Then (Effie) kisses us each on the cheek and hurries out" (p. 138).
"In the fall, a few brave souls sneak into the woods to harvest apples" (p. 6).
Discussed in Chapter: 7
Another Grammatical Concept in this Text: Eliminating wordiness through specific noun use
Related Common Core Standard: L7.3
Excerpts that Demonstrate Concept:
"Sometimes, when I clean a kill, I feed Buttercup the entrails" (p. 4).
"The hovercraft appears a hundred yards or so away" (p. 318).
"I finally had to kill the lynx because he scared off game" (p. 7).
Discussed in Chapter: 7

DuPrau, J. (2003). *The city of ember.* New York, NY: Random House Books for Young Readers.
Title: *The City of Ember*
Author: Jeanne DuPrau
Grammatical Concept: Complex sentences
Related Common Core Standard: L7.1

Excerpt that Demonstrates Concept:
"When Lina went to work the next morning, the street was oddly silent" (p. 84).
Discussed in Chapter: 5

Gratz, A. (2017). *Refugee.* New York, NY: Scholastic.
Title: *Refugee*
Author: Alan Gratz
Grammatical concept: Using phrases and clauses while recognizing and correcting dangling modifiers
Related Common Core Standard: L7.1
Excerpt that Demonstrates Concept:
"She played it salsa for her mother and her father, who had left their homeland, and for her little brother Mariano, who would never know the streets of Havana the way she had" (p. 308).
Discussed in Chapter: 6

Grimes, N. (2002). *Bronx masquerade.* New York, NY: Dial Books.
Title: *Bronx Masquerade*
Author: Nikki Grimes
Grammatical Concept: Maintaining consistency in style and tone
Related Common Core Standard: L6.3
Excerpt that Demonstrates Concept:
"Future? What I got is right here, right now, spending time with my homeys. Wish there was some future to talk about. I could use me some future" (p. 8).
Discussed in Chapter: 4
Another Grammatical Concept in this Text: Verb moods
Related Common Core Standard: L8.1
Excerpts that Demonstrate Concept:
"I've been drawing pictures all my life" (p. 20) (example of indicative mood).
"Don't call me Jump Shot" (p. 32) (example of imperative mood).
"Lupe, what's wrong?" (p. 66) (example of interrogative mood).
"Tyrone might convince everyone else he's all through with dreaming, but I know he wants to be a big hip-hop star" (p. 3) (example of conditional mood).
"If I had moves like Devon, I'd be cruising crosscourt with Scottie Pippin!" (p. 33) (example of subjunctive mood).
Discussed in Chapter: 11

Horowitz, A. (2000). *Stormbreaker*. New York, NY: Speak.
Title: *Stormbreaker*
Author: Anthony Horowitz
Grammatical Concept: Using proper pronoun case
Related Common Core Standard: L6.1
Excerpts that Demonstrate Concept:
"He took out a pair of Gap combat trousers, Nike sweatshirt and sneakers, got dressed, then sat on the bed and waited" (p. 33) (example of subjective case).
"Alex opened his eyes" (p. 32) (example of possessive case).
"Nobody followed him" (p. 22) (example of objective case).
Discussed in Chapter: 2

Khan, H. (2017). *Amina's voice*. New York, NY: Salaam Reads.
Title: *Amina's Voice*
Author: Hena Khan
Grammatical Concept: Intensive pronoun use
Related Common Core Standard: L6.1
Excerpt that Demonstrates Concept:
"Mama told me once that she picked my name thinking it would be easiest of all the ones on her list for people in America to pronounce. But she was wrong. The neighbor with the creepy cat still calls me Amelia after living next door for five years. And my last name? Forget about it. I could barely pronounce Khokar myself until I was eight" (p. 10).
Discussed in Chapter: 1

London, J. (1906). *The call of the wild, White Fang, and other stories*. New York, NY: Penguin.
Title (of Discussed Text): *White Fang*
Author: Jack London
Grammatical Concept: Using phrases and clauses while recognizing and correcting dangling modifiers
Related Common Core Standard: L7.1
Excerpts that Demonstrate Concept:
"The wolf-dogs, clustered on the far side of the fire, snarled and bickered among themselves, but evinced no inclination to stray off in the darkness" (p. 172).
"A few minutes later, Henry, who was now traveling behind the sled, emitted a low, warning whistle" (p. 185).
Discussed in Chapter: 6

Myers, W.D. (1999). *Monster.* New York, NY: HarperCollins.
Title: *Monster*
Author: Walter Dean Myers
Grammatical Concept: Using proper pronoun case
Related Common Core Standard: L6.1
Excerpt that Demonstrates Concept:
"I wouldn't lie in court" (p. 104) (example of subjective case).
Discussed in Chapter: 2

Myers, W.D. (2001). *Bad boy.* New York, NY: HarperCollins.
Title: *Bad Boy*
Author: Walter Dean Myers
Grammatical Concept: Using proper pronoun case
Related Common Core Standard: L6.1
Excerpt that Demonstrates Concept:
"I traveled, mostly with Mama, to other parts of the city, but nothing matched Harlem" (p. 48) (example of subjective case).
Discussed in Chapter: 2

Napoli, D.J. (1998). *Sirena.* New York, NY: Scholastic.
Title: *Sirena*
Author: Donna Jo Napoli
Grammatical Concept: Using phrases and clauses while recognizing and correcting dangling modifiers
Related Common Core Standard: L7.1
Excerpts that Demonstrate Concept:
"Our island, which was once a mass of fragrant yellow lilies, has become an open graveyard" (p. 19).
"Philoctetes gets up and goes to his wooden chest, dug halfway into the ground among the bushes" (p. 116).
Discussed in Chapter: 6

Noah, T. (2019). *It's Trevor Noah: Born a crime. Stories from a South African Childhood. Adapted for young readers.* New York, NY: Delacorte Press.
Title: *It's Trevor Noah: Born a Crime. Stories from a South African Childhood. Adapted for Young Readers.*
Author: Trevor Noah
Grammatical Concept: Using punctuation to indicate a pause or break
Related Common Core Standard: L8.2

Excerpts that Demonstrate Concept:
"When the colonial armies invaded, the Zulu charged into battle with nothing but spears and shields against men with guns" (p. 3).
"If the person who doesn't look like you speaks like you, your brain short-circuits: the racism code of 'if he doesn't look like me he isn't like me' suddenly smashes against the language code of 'if he speaks like me he…is like me'" (p. 50)
"Apartheid—the South African government policy of racial segregation—was genius at convincing people who were the overwhelming majority to turn on each other" (p. 3).
Discussed in Chapter: 12

Phelan, M.K. (1976). *The story of the Boston Massacre.* New York, NY: Thomas Y. Crowell.
Title: *The Story of the Boston Massacre*
Author: Mary Kay Phelan
Grammatical Concept: Maintaining consistency in style and tone
Related Common Core Standard: L6.3
Excerpt that Demonstrates Concept:
"The law-making body is composed of two houses: the Council, or upper house, and the Assembly, or lower house" (p. 15).
Discussed in Chapter: 4

Pitman, G.E. (2019). *The Stonewall Riots: Coming out in the streets.* New York, NY: Abrams Books for Young Readers.
Title: *The Stonewall Riots: Coming Out in the Streets*
Author: Gayle E. Pitman
Grammatical Concept: Using punctuation to set off nonrestrictive elements
Related Common Core Standard: L6.2
Excerpts that Demonstrate Concept:
"Rita Mae Brown, a lesbian who also identified as a feminist, had difficulty finding a group that addressed all aspects of her identity" (p. 135).
"In the end, 103 people (89 men and 14 women) were arrested and taken to jail" (p. 22).
"The person who led the chant was Craig Rodwell, a gay activist and owner of the Oscar Wilde Memorial Bookshop—the first gay bookstore in the United States" (p. 69).
Discussed in Chapter: 3

Saeed, A. (2018). *Amal unbound.* New York, NY: Nancy Paulsen Books.
Title: *Amal Unbound*
Author: Aisha Saeed

Grammatical Concept: Verbals (gerunds, participles, and infinitives)
Related Common Core Standard: L8.1
Excerpts that Demonstrate Concept:
"I loved watching her go over her lessons and rework them based on what worked and what didn't the day before" (p. 3) (example of gerund).
"The sun blazed overhead, warming my chador and my hair beneath it" (p. 6) (example of participle).
"I wanted to be a teacher when I grew up…" (p. 3) (example of infinitive).
"We lined up by the chalkboard at the front of the class to get our tests" (p. 2) (example of infinitive).
Discussed in Chapter: 9

Snicket, L. (1999). *The bad beginning.* New York, NY: HarperCollins.
Title: *The Bad Beginning*
Author: Lemony Snicket
Grammatical Concept: Maintaining consistency in style and tone
Related Common Core Standard: L6.3
Excerpt that Demonstrates Concept:
"If you are interested in stories with happy endings, you would be better off reading some other book. In this book, not only is there no happy ending, there is no happy beginning and very few happy things happen in the middle" (p. 1).
Discussed in Chapter: 4

Sotomayor, S. (2018). *The beloved world of Sonia Sotomayor.* New York, NY: Delacorte Press.
Title: *The Beloved World of Sonia Sotomayor*
Author: Sonia Sotomayor
Grammatical Concept: Language that expresses ideas precisely and eliminates wordiness and redundancy
Related Common Core Standard: L7.3
Excerpts that Demonstrate Concept:
"I was a watchful child constantly scanning the adults for clues and listening in on their conversations" (p. 18).
"When my father made his first attempt at giving me the insulin shot the day before, his hands were shaking so much I was afraid he would miss my arm and stab me in the face" (p. 5).
Discussed in Chapter: 7

Strasser, T. (1981). *The wave.* New York, NY: Bantam Doubleday Dell.
Title: *The Wave*
Author: Todd Strasser

Grammatical Concept: Connotation
Related Common Core Standard: L7.5
Excerpt that Demonstrates Concept:
"On weekends he'd visit Indian reservations or spend hours looking for old books in dusty libraries" (p. 33).
Discussed in Chapter: 8

Takei, G. (2019). *They called us enemy.* Marietta, GA: Top Shelf Productions.
Title: *They Called Us Enemy*
Author: George Takei
Grammatical Concept: Simple sentence
Related Common Core Standard: L7.1
Excerpt that Demonstrates Concept:
"My parents met in California" (p. 11).
Discussed in Chapter: 5
Another Grammatical Concept in this Text: Compound sentence
Related Common Core Standard: L7.1
Excerpt that Demonstrates Concept:
"He would call her Mama from then on, and she would call him Daddy" (p. 12).
Discussed in Chapter: 5
Another Grammatical Concept in this Text: Complex sentence
Related Common Core Standard: L7.1
Excerpt that Demonstrates Concept:
"Whenever we would approach a town, we were forced to draw the shade" (p. 40).
Discussed in Chapter: 5
Another Grammatical Concept in this Text: Compound-complex sentence
Related Common Core Standard: L7.1
Excerpt that Demonstrates Concept:
"After he was attacked, the people of Manzanar assumed they'd seen the last of Herbert … but sure enough, the next month on that same date, Herbert was back at Manzanar with more books" (p. 146–147).
Discussed in Chapter: 5

Westerfield, S. (2004). *Midnighters: The secret hour.* New York, NY: HarperCollins.
Title: *Midnighters: The Secret Hour*
Author: Scott Westerfield
Grammatical Concept: Connotation

Excerpt that Demonstrates Concept:
"It wasn't just the unfamiliar house; the Oklahoma night itself felt wrong" (p. 16).
Discussed in Chapter: 8

Woodson, J. (2000). *Miracle's boys.* New York, NY: Speak.
Title: *Miracle's Boys*
Author: Jacqueline Woodson
Grammatical Concept: Verb moods
Related Common Core Standard: L8.1
Excerpts that Demonstrate Concept:
"You thinking about Mama?" (p. 28) (example of interrogative mood).
"I lay back on my bed and listened to my brother Newcharlie talking" (p. 1) (example of indicative mood).
"Charlie, don't cry. Please don't cry" (p. 41). (example of imperative mood).
Discussed in Chapter: 11

Zusak, M. (2005). *The book thief.* New York, NY: Alfred A. Knopf.
Title: *The Book Thief*
Author: Markus Zusak
Grammatical Concept: Using punctuation to indicate a pause or break
Related Common Core Standard: L8.2
Excerpts that Demonstrate Concept:
"If he's turned into a Nazi—which is very likely—I'll just turn around" (p. 125).
"When it came to stealing, Liesel and Rudy first stuck with the idea that there was safety in numbers" (p. 272).
Discussed in Chapter: 12

References

Avi. (1990). *The true confessions of Charlotte Doyle*. New York, NY: Harper Trophy.

Barnes, D. (1992). *From communication to curriculum*. Portsmouth, NH: Boyton/Cook.

Berman, L. (2009). *The greatest moments in sports*. Naperville, IL: Sourcebooks Jabberwocky.

Brooks, B. (1994). *Predator*. New York, NY: Farrar, Straus, & Giroux.

Bruns, R. (2000). *Billy the Kid: Outlaw of the Wild West*. Berkeley Heights, NJ: Enslow.

Cartaya, P. (2017). *The epic fail of Arturo Zamora*. New York, NY: Puffin Books.

Clements, A. (2002). *Things not seen*. New York, NY: Puffin Books.

Collier, J. L., & Collier, C. (1974). *My brother Sam is dead*. New York, NY: Scholastic.

Collins, S. (2008). *The hunger games*. New York, NY: Scholastic.

Common Core State Standards Initiative (2010). *Common core state standards for English language arts*. Retrieved from: www.corestandards.org/ELA-Literacy.

DuPrau, J. (2003). *The city of ember*. New York, NY: Random House Books for Young Readers.

Fisher, D., & Frey, N. (2003). Writing instruction for struggling adolescent readers: A gradual release model. *Journal of Adolescent & Adult Literacy, 46*(5), 396–407.

Fletcher, R., & Portalupi, J. (2001). *Writing workshop: The essential guide*. Portsmouth, NH: Heinemann.

Gratz, A. (2017). *Refugee*. New York, NY: Scholastic.

Green, J. (2006). *An abundance of Katherines*. New York, NY: Speak.

Grimes, N. (2002). *Bronx masquerade*. New York, NY: Dial Books.

Gruwell, E., & The Freedom Writers. (1999). *The freedom writers diary*. New York, NY: Broadway Books.

Harvey, S., & Goudvis, A. (2007). *Strategies that work: Teaching comprehension for understanding and engagement* (2nd ed.). Portland, ME: Stenhouse.

Horowitz, A. (2000). *Stormbreaker*. New York, NY: Speak.

Khan, H. (2017). *Amina's voice*. New York, NY: Salaam Reads.

Killgallon, D., & Killgallon, J. (2010). *Grammar for college writing: A sentence-composing approach*. Portsmouth, NH: Heinemann.

Kolln, M., & Funk, R. (2012). *Understanding English grammar* (9th ed.). New York, NY: Pearson.

Lloyd, S. L. (2004). Using comprehension strategies as a springboard for student talk. *Journal of Adolescent & Adult Literacy, 48*(2), 114–124.

London, J. (1906). *The call of the wild, White Fang, and other stories*. New York, NY: Penguin.

Mass, W. (2004). *Leap day*. New York, NY: Time Warner Book Group.

Myers, W. D. (1988). *Fallen angels*. New York, NY: Scholastic.

Myers, W. D. (1999). *Monster*. New York, NY: HarperCollins.

Myers, W. D. (2001). *Bad boy*. New York, NY: HarperCollins.

Napoli, D. J. (1998). *Sirena*. New York, NY: Scholastic.

National Council of Teachers of English (2016). *Professional knowledge for the teaching of writing*. Retrieved from https://ncte.org/statement/teaching-writing/.

National Council of Teachers of English (2018). *Statement on gender and language*. Retrieved from www2.ncte.org/statement/genderfairuseoflang/.

Noah, T. (2019). *It's Trevor Noah: Born a crime. Stories from a South African childhood. Aapted for young readers*. New York, NY: Delacorte Press.

Pearson, P. D., & Gallagher, M. C. (1983). The instruction of reading comprehension. *Contemporary Education Psychology, 8*, 317–344.

Phelan, M. K. (1976). *The story of the Boston Massacre*. New York, NY: Thomas Y. Crowell.

Pitman, G. E. (2019). *The Stonewall Riots: Coming out in the streets*. New York, NY: Abrams Books for Young Readers.

Pullman, P. (1996). *Clockwork*. New York, NY: Scholastic.

Robb, L. (2010). *Teaching middle school writers: What every English teacher needs to know*. Portsmouth, NH: Heinemann.

Saeed, A. (2018). *Amal unbound*. New York, NY: Nancy Paulsen Books.

Shannon, D. (2004). *A bad case of stripes*. New York, NY: Scholastic.

Snicket, L. (1999). *The bad beginning*. New York, NY: HarperCollins.

Soto, G. (1993). Push up. In G. Soto, *Local news* (pp. 47–59). New York, NY: Scholastic.

Sotomayor, S. (2018). *The beloved world of Sonia Sotomayor*. New York, NY: Delacorte Press.

Strasser, T. (1981). *The wave*. New York, NY: Bantam Doubleday Dell.

Strunk, W., & White, E. B. (1959). *The elements of style*. New York, NY: Macmillan.

Takei, G. (2019). *They called us enemy*. Marietta, GA: Top Shelf Productions.

Weaver, C. (1998). Teaching grammar in the context of writing. In C. Weaver (Ed.), *Lessons to share on teaching grammar in context* (pp. 18–38). Portsmouth, NH: Boynton/Cook.

Westerfield, S. (2004). *Midnighters: The secret hour*. New York, NY: HarperCollins.

Wilhelm, J. D. (2001). *Improving comprehension with think-aloud strategies*. New York, NY: Scholastic.

Woodson, J. (2000). *Miracle's boys*. New York, NY: Speak.

Zinsser, W. (2006). *On writing well: 30th anniversary edition*. New York, NY: Harper Perennial.

Zusak, M. (2005). *The book thief*. New York, NY: Alfred A. Knopf.

Appendix

Reproducible Charts and Forms You Can Use in Your Classroom

Original Sentence	Sentence without Intensive Pronouns	How They Differ

Figure 1.2 Sentences with and without Intensive Pronouns.

Copyright 2014 Taylor & Francis. All rights reserved. www.routledge.com

Sentence	Intensive Pronoun	Why the Intensive Pronoun Is Important to the Sentence

Figure 1.3 Sentence Analysis chart.

Copyright 2014 Taylor & Francis. All rights reserved. www.routledge.com

Sentence	Pronoun and its Case	Why the Author Used that Case

Figure 2.4 Chart for Pronoun Case Analysis.

Original Sentence	Sentence Revised to Include Nonrestrictive Element	Nonrestrictive Element You Added	Punctuation Used with Nonrestrictive Element

Figure 3.3 Graphic Organizer for Nonrestrictive Elements.

Copyright 2014 Taylor & Francis. All rights reserved. www.routledge.com

Original Text	The Text's Tone	How the Author Created this Tone	Your Revised Version of this Text	The Text's Tone	How You Created this Tone

Figure 4.3 Tone Comparison Chart.

Copyright 2014 Taylor & Francis. All rights reserved. www.routledge.com

Sentence that Stood Out to You as Effective	Sentence Type	Sentence Rewritten as Another Type	What Would Be Different if the Sentence was Written this Way?

Figure 5.6 Sentence Type Analysis Chart.

Copyright 2014 Taylor & Francis. All rights reserved. www.routledge.com

Sentence with a Specific Noun	Rewritten Sentence with the Specific Noun Replaced by a Vague Noun and an Adjective	How You Think the Sentences Are Different

Figure 7.3 Specific Noun Sentence Chart.

Sentence with a Strong Verb	Rewritten Sentence with the Strong Verb Replaced by a Weak Verb and an Adverb	How You Think the Sentences Are Different

Figure 7.4 Strong Verb Sentence Chart.

Copyright 2014 Taylor & Francis. All rights reserved. www.routledge.com

Original Sentence	Sentence with a Word Replaced by Another with a Different Connotation	How the Connotations of Those Words Differ

Figure 8.4 Model for Connotation Replacement.

Copyright 2014 Taylor & Francis. All rights reserved. www.routledge.com

Appendix ◆ 203

Sentence from Published Text	Verbal in the Sentence	Kind of Verbal it Is

Figure 9.1 Chart for Students to Use in Verbal "Scavenger Hunt" Activity.

Copyright 2014 Taylor & Francis. All rights reserved. www.routledge.com

Sentence in Active Voice	Changed to Passive Voice	Analysis of the Differences

Figure 10.1 Chart for Active/Passive Voice Activity.

Copyright 2014 Taylor & Francis. All rights reserved. www.routledge.com

Sentence	Mood	Why You Think the Author Used this Mood

Figure 11.1 Verb Mood in Literature Chart.

Copyright 2014 Taylor & Francis. All rights reserved. www.routledge.com

Sentences You Found that Use Punctuation to Indicate a Pause or Break	Type of Punctuation Used for this Purpose	Why this Punctuation Is Important to the Sentence

Figure 12.3 Chart to Use When Finding Examples from Literature of Punctuation that Indicates a Pause or Break.

Copyright 2014 Taylor & Francis. All rights reserved. www.routledge.com